THE SPIRITUAL MALADY

HOW TO ATTAIN PEACE OF MIND AND LASTING HAPPINESS

REN KOI

www.dwyctoday.com

With all my love, I dedicate this book to
my daughter Alice
xx

THANKS

I'm very grateful to my mum and dad, my fiancée Adele, my daughter Alice, my step-children Lillian and Isobel, my dog Teddy, my sponsor Alex, Barbarah H, Ben Piper, Michelle D, David M, Mark C, Kate Lambert, Jonathan Bagshaw, Shaun Marriot, Adam McGuire, Stuart N, all my fellows in Twelve Step fellowships, and all my family and friends.

**PEACE
AND
LOVE**

CHAPTERS

THE FIRST LESSON: PATIENCE
SIMPLIFYING ADDICTION
CLIMBING THE MOUNTAIN
SHROOM

LESSON TWO: IMPERMENANCE
ELAN VITAL
MICHELLE'S STORY

LESSON THREE: PRIDE
HUMILITY IS NOT HUMILIATION
EMOTIONAL INTELLIGENCE
SURRENDER TO WIN

LESSON FOUR: TURNING IT OVER
HELP! I NEED SOMEBODY
MARK'S STORY

LESSON FIVE: EGO-DEFLATION
SHAME AND GUILT AND BLAME
THE ANCIENT DISCIPLINE OF CONFESSION

LESSON SIX: CHANGE
EGO-ALARM
THE SELF-FORGETFULNESS OF ALTRUISM

LESSON SEVEN: ATONEMENT
MAKING AMENDS
MATTHEW'S STORY

LESSON EIGHT: EQUINIMITY
FORGIVENESS AND TRUST
CHECK YOURSELF BEFORE YOU WRECK YOURSELF

"WHEN THE SPIRITUAL MALADY IS OVERCOME, WE STRAIGHTEN OUT MENTALLY AND PHYSICALLY"

– Alcoholics Anonymous (Big Book)

FOREWORD

When Ren asked me to write the foreword to this book, I was delighted to do so... as it also takes you through my journey from addiction to recovery.

My name is Barbara and I'm an alcoholic and compulsive overeater... in recovery. I haven't drunk alcohol since 01/01/2007 or compulsively eaten since 03/03/2010... one day at a time. Each day being a daily reprieve from a crippling physical, mental, emotional, spiritual, compulsive, and progressive dis-ease.

Ren describes in detail and very eloquently what we are all looking for... (whether we know it or not)... peace of mind. Not for the future, but for today. It was the famous psychoanalyst Erich Fromm who said, "Man is the only animal for whom his own existence is a problem which he has to solve."

Most of us get caught up in the web of daily living – it's ups and downs – highs and lows... and the emotional turmoil that usually goes with it. Ren discusses the tenets of The Twelve Step Program and how it is transforming his life. Being part of his journey has been very rewarding and has strengthened my own recovery. I have been so blessed in my journey from insanity to sanity that I haven't had to walk it alone, as it is so easy to isolate. As spiritual teacher and former clinical psychologist Ram Dass says, "We are all just walking each other home."

But what is peace of mind?... For me, and also as Ren shares in this book... it really is quite simple. It's about letting go of the resistance to life's flow. From the early days of my recovery, the words of contemporary spiritual teacher Eckhart Tolle sum it up nicely and will stay with me forever, "Non-resistance, non-judgement and non-attachment are the keys for successful living."

This book is about courage. It takes courage to look at your 'character defects' that block, 'the sunlight of the spirit,' and keep you in the same conditioned patterns of behavior. A willingness to change is such a gift. A new way of living is possible – of acting on life – rather than reacting to it.

I am so very grateful to Ren for his unique insight and working knowledge of The Twelve Steps. He makes them accessible and relatable. This book has reminded me that life doesn't have to be complicated... 'Keep It Simple' being one of the Twelve Step mantras by which I live my life.

Barbarah H

INTRODUCTION

If you don't find life easy – in fact you find life difficult and challenging – this book is for you. If you prefer peace of mind and contentment to a chaotic and unmanageable mind that manifests misery, this book is definitely for you. I'm no authority on peace of mind or happiness but I can attest to being cognitively chaotic, emotionally unmanageable, and unhappy most of my adult life until I had a spiritual awakening in 2009 and set off on a journey, which, ten years on, has brought me contentment – as a result of a peaceful mind.

My spiritual awakening was a moment of grace, and grace, as I understand it, is the speeding up of a person's return to God, which is where we are all heading anyway in my opinion. By 'spiritual awakening,' I simply mean becoming aware of, and dis-identifying with, my ego-mind – while simultaneously and progressively identifying more with my heart-mind (which I discuss in more detail in the last chapter). This 'psychic change' or 'quantum shift' is a continual dis-identification process with one's ego-mind, which evolves as one becomes more self-aware.

I don't have peace of mind all the time of course and I still use substances, such as chocolate, and behaviors, such as shopping, to soothe my emotional dis-ease, but my happiness levels have increased year-on-year since I began my recovery from addiction in 2009. If I had to quantify it, I'd say (at the time of publishing in March 2020) approximately 80% of the time I'm content, 10% of the time I'm joyous, 5% of the time I have a low mood, 4% of the time I'm anxious, and very rarely am I completely miserable, which I think is pretty good-going in today's world! I would strongly argue that contentment, from which happiness and joy arise sporadically, is directly proportionate to peace of mind. If I have a peaceful mind I can't be restless, irritable, or discontent, and therefore I can't be unhappy – no matter my circumstances.

Today, I think a small but growing percentage of people feel a tangible sense of despair about their lives and the fate of the planet, and a huge percentage of people feel a general sense of dissatisfaction or dis-ease. This is why the vast majority of people use 'fixes,' such as food, drugs (including alcohol and cigarettes), shopping, exercise, sex, work, TV, and social media unwittingly to change the way they feel – from a restless, irritable, or discontented state – to a state of orchestrated contentment. We call it 'taking our comfort,' or, in the case of food, 'comfort eating,' but the comfort experienced from any of the substances or behaviors mentioned above is usually fleeting and the dis-ease always returns. If you asked the vast majority of people in the western world to just sit in silence and 'be' – with no external stimuli at all – most people wouldn't be able to last any longer than a couple of minutes (some even less).

I began practicing meditation in 2013 and I'm now able to sit for up to eight hours per day, one hour at a time, as demonstrated when I attended a ten-day Vipassana (translating to 'insight' or 'inward vision') silent meditation retreat in September 2018. This is how I would benchmark peace of mind: an ability to just 'be' without any need to reach for a drink, a cigarette, the TV remote, mobile phone, laptop or tablet, or have music playing. Obviously peace of mind is subjective, but I think most people would agree it is generally recognized as a state of serenity and not wanting, desiring, craving, or fearing anything in the present moment. In fact, every want, desire, craving, or fear takes you immediately out of the present moment and into the past or future, which moves you away from peace of mind toward low mood, excitement, or anxiety. Generally speaking, sad and depressed people have one thing in common: they all live in the past. Anxious and fearful people have one thing in common: they all live in the future. And happy and joyful people also have one thing in common: they all live in the present. Peace, therefore, is actually peace *from* mind rather than peace *of* mind, as it is the ego-mind continuously flitting from past to future that creates our misery.

Meditation and mindfulness (defused, accepting, and open contact with the present moment) are ultimately how I cultivate peace of mind and contentment. I didn't mention my mediocre meditation capacity with any sense of ego, or as a way of 'peacocking.' I've simply stated this fact to emphasize that I, who was once unstable as an active alcoholic/addict, emotionally and mentally unwell, and unable to sit in silence for more than a few seconds, am now in recovery from what the original Twelve Step fellowship Alcoholics Anonymous terms, "The Spiritual Malady," and able to sit and observe my ego-mind, and my emotional state, with equanimity. The word 'malady' means illness, disease, or serious problem, and I believe 'The Spiritual Malady' is at the root of all human suffering, including addictions.

This book was written as a result of attending the aforementioned meditation retreat. It has been put together as a series of lessons that I've learned over the past ten years since I started to develop peace of mind – after I began my recovery journey and changed – progressively realizing that a materialistic life is inherently nihilistic and that I must develop my own sense of purpose and meaning that isn't centered around *more* (more money, more power, more control, more clothes, more sex, more food, ad-infinitum).

My first Twelve Step sponsor/mentor told me that things don't get better by chance, they get better by change, and there's only one thing I needed to change, and that thing is *me*. He explained that I didn't have to change everything over-night but, if I wanted my circumstances to change, and if I wanted to remain 'clean and sober' and live a life of meaning, I'd have to look at changing *all* my selfish, self-seeking, dishonest, and fearful behaviors, as they were clearly not serving me or anyone else. I couldn't argue with him at the time and I still can't argue with what he said.

With my continual evolution, an ever-progressing serenity and peace of mind has emerged, and as a result I am progressively happier; living a simple and humble life with my fiancée Adele, my daughter Alice, my two step-daughters Lillian and Isobel, my dog Teddy, and my wider family and friends. I enjoy a life beyond my wildest dreams that I could never have imagined, as all I ever wanted to be from the age of 16 to 28 – when I was an active alcoholic – was a famous DJ. Instead, I gave up the addictive chase for success, fame, and fortune, which took me from Manchester to London via Leeds, Newcastle, Australia, and Gran Canaria, in favor of a family life in the suburbs of Birmingham. I could never have written the script but I'm so glad I couldn't see what my Higher Power had planned for me.

Twelve Step fellowships prescribe abstinence (from substances and/or compulsive behaviors) and a Higher Power (of your own understanding) as the solution to addiction. Abstinence from fixations, desires, cravings, and attractions is, I believe, the key to a peaceful mind. There is currently no recognized cure for addiction, there are only psychotropic medications, such as Librium (chlordiazepoxide) for alcohol addiction and Physeptone (methadone) or Buprenorphine (Subutex) for opioid addiction, plus a plethora of anti-anxiety and anti-depressant medications that people use to treat their symptoms. All of which merely substitute dependence in my opinion, especially if there is no plan in place for the person to exit treatment.

Psychotropic medications are designed to make you not feel your feelings but you can't selectively numb your feelings; if you numb your pain you also numb your joy. In order to live a fulfilled human life, I believe the aim is to feel *all* your feelings, so you can experience sadness, depression, and anxiety when appropriate, and pleasure, happiness, and joy when appropriate. Unlike The Twelve Step Program, psychotropic drugs medicate symptoms but they do provide a solution to The Spiritual Malady at the root of all suffering. This is where a Higher Power (of your own understanding) comes in to play.

When I talk or write about my 'Higher Power,' I am referring to Consciousness, which I believe pervades all things, therefore, Consciousness is God. Communion with my Higher Power happens through connection; connection to my innermost self (Consciousness), vulnerable connection to other people, and connection to nature, which is essentially my church. Connection is also how I progressively overcome alcoholism. "The opposite of addiction is not sobriety. The opposite of addiction is connection," according to Johann Hari, author of the New York Times best-selling book, *Chasing The Scream: The First and Last*

Days of the War on Drugs, which is a statement I wholeheartedly agree with.

I'm certainly not trying to push my conception of a Higher Power on you, I'm simply suggesting that you will need real, deep connections with other people (and nature) if you're going to achieve lasting peace of mind and contentment. The genius of The Twelve Step Program is it gives you autonomy to choose your own Higher Power, which removes any notion of prescription to a religion or philosophy.

Ever since I tentatively became open-minded to the idea that a Higher Power might be working in my life, I've gone from strength to strength, as I was gifted a new strength, courage, and Power not normally my own. In 2014 I left my secure, highly-paid, but unfulfilling and soul-destroying sales career in London and moved to Gran Canaria to find my true calling. This led me back to London to pursue a helping career that led me to work as a Drug and Alcohol Counsellor in UK prisons for four years. I now enjoy leading the Homeless Team for a community-based substance misuse service, and I also record the *Life in Recovery Podcast* and write books in my spare time. I've found that my passion and purpose is to spread a message of love and service, which I learned from Twelve Step fellowships – where I also learned the importance of connection.

American psychiatrist and best-selling author M. Scott Peck suggested in his book *Further Along The Road Less Travelled,* that the real reason Twelve Step fellowships work is because of 'The Program.' He wrote that the first reason The Program works is because The Twelve Steps are the only existing program for 'spiritual conversion.' The second reason is that it's a psychological program, which teaches people not only why to go forward through the 'desert' toward God but also a great deal about how to go forward. One way The Program teaches is through aphorisms and proverbs such as, 'the only person you can change is yourself,' and, 'one day at a time.' The second is a system of sponsors. He explains that a sponsor is really a lay-psychotherapist and there's something of a tradition in The Twelve Step Program that it's okay to outgrow your sponsor. He therefore believes the sponsor system superior to traditional therapy, as there are not many psychiatrists who would take kindly to their patients' outgrowing them. I agree with M. Scott Peck's sentiments and I also believe Twelve Step fellowships work because they teach people they don't have to go forward through the desert alone. It's a community program, and community (sangha in the Buddhist tradition) often develops naturally in response to suffering and crisis, in which all chronic addicts eventually find themselves.

For the record, I prefer the term 'substance and/or behavioral dependent,' but for ease of reference I refer to myself and other people who are addicted to substances (including alcohol) and/or behaviors as 'addicts.' A 'chronic addict,' therefore, is someone who has suffered from the disease of addiction for a long time and is dependent on a substance and/or behavior.

I feel the whole world is progressively becoming more addicted as a result of the universal Spiritual Malady. Unfortunately (or fortunately as it may come to pass), it seems the planet and its inhabitants are entering a period of ecological and moral crisis – brought to our attention by media outlets reporting on: homelessness, a rise in crime, terrorism, mass shootings, ecological disasters, the global mental health crisis, and the global (pharmaceutical, illicit substance, and behavioral) addiction epidemic, which is inextricably linked to poor mental and emotional health. Thanks especially to social media, many of these reports are no longer skewed by political agendas, and the facts, although sometimes difficult to discern, are available for all to see. We are clearly in the midst of a spiritual crisis – moving us further and further away from peace of mind and contentment toward a global 'rock-bottom' – and we need a solution. The great news is, there is a solution, and that's what this book is all about.

Currently it feels like we're in the Garden of Eden and Hell simultaneously – not only in our own minds but also in the material world. Although we live in an age of immense technological and material achievement and advancement, we have yet to overcome homelessness (which is on the rise in the west and is now recognized as a mental health issue as much as a housing issue) and poverty (globally). The disparity between rich and poor continues to increase exponentially, which I believe is directly related to an innate need for control and an anti-spiritual addiction to power and material satisfactions.

At work, I'm faced with spiritual crisis and some of the worst human suffering (literally 'Hell on Earth') on a daily basis, as my team help Birmingham's homeless community with their substance misuse and physical and mental health issues. A less obvious but regular example in my personal life is, when I'm out walking my dog on the local common, I'm moved by the beauty of nature yet simultaneously saddened by all the litter everywhere. Thanks to the Vipassana meditation retreat, however, I now know inherently that all my suffering is caused by either my desires (craving), my aversions (fear), or my ignorance (things I don't know or understand). In these particular cases, my suffering is caused by my desire to end poverty and homelessness and my aversion to litter. In response to my suffering, I simply do what I can by doing my best at work each day and picking up the litter as often as I can, which I would say is the 'spiritual' thing to do, as it gives me peace of mind.

I want to make it clear from the outset that I am not a religious man, and I believe there is a huge difference between religion and spirituality. In my opinion, religion is analogous to a fish in a fishbowl, whereas spirituality is analogous to a fish in the ocean. Religion seems mainly to be for those people who want to reach paradise and avoid pain and suffering in an afterlife, whereas spirituality is for those people who want to transform their pain and suffering into peace of mind and happiness in this life. I find that truly spiritual people have already been to hell and, "walked out of the flames carrying buckets of water for those still consumed by the fire," to quote American R&B singer Stephanie Sparkles. I agree, therefore, with American author and ayurvedic doctor, Robert E. Svoboda, who wrote in *Aghora: At the Left Hand of God*, "I have never believed in religion. Religions are all limited because they concentrate only on one aspect of truth. That is why they are always fighting amongst one another because they all think they are in the sole possession of the truth.

But I say, there is no end to knowledge, so there is no use in trying to confine it to one scripture, or one Holy book, or one experience. That is why I say, when people ask me what religion I follow, I believe in incineration; burn down everything that is getting in the way of your perception of the truth."

So let's put religion to one side, and for the remainder of this book I ask you to remain completely open-minded about spirituality. I invite you to consider that you are not a 'human being' but a 'spiritual being' (Consciousness) having a human experience and that no system that is divorced from spirituality (be it education, work, entertainment, or politics), will ever bring you contentment. Change, therefore, is essential, as most aspects of our lives are becoming ever-more divorced from spirituality due to the continual and progressive secularism of modern society. Change starts with each and every one of us. We can only ever change ourselves – but if we change en masse – society will change. Perhaps our current spiritual, moral, and ecological crisis will be the catalyst for this much needed change? Only time will tell...

I also ask you to consider, that which we commonly refer to as 'God' (what legendary Greek philosopher Aristotle and later the influential Italian Catholic Priest St. Thomas Aquinas referred to as the "Unmoved Mover" or the "Prime Mover"), is what Swiss psychoanalyst Carl Jung referred to as "One world" (the concept of an underlying unified reality from which everything emerges and to which everything returns), and New Age author, Deepak Chopra describes as an, "Infinite Field of Possibility." God, therefore, might be the Source field comprising the whole universe that we now most commonly refer to as 'Consciousness.' Renowned Advaita (translating to 'One Source'; a school of Hindu philosophy believed to be a classic path to spiritual realization) master Ramesh Balsekar said, "All there is, is Consciousness."

Hungarian-American theoretical physicist and mathematician, Eugene Wigner, who was a contemporary of theoretical physicist, Albert Einstein, said that physics can't even prove physics, and it wasn't possible to formulate the laws of quantum theory in a fully consistent way without reference to Consciousness. Consultant and editor for books about neuroscience and physics, Annaka Harris, who is the wife of infamous 'New Atheist,' philosopher, neuroscientist, and author, Sam Harris, introduced 'Panpsychism' (the idea that everything material, however small, has an element of individual Consciousness) in her 2019 book, *Conscious: A Brief Guide to the Fundamental Mystery of the Mind*. Panpsychism is a concept long present in spiritual and metaphysical schools of thought, and only more recently embraced by a handful of physicists. According to Scientific Director of Advanced Cell Technology Company, Dr. Robert Lanza, Biocentrism also teaches us that Consciousness creates the material universe, not the other way around. Lanza points to the structure of the universe itself, and that the laws, forces, and constants of the universe appear to be fine-tuned for life, implying intelligence existed prior to matter – with Consciousness being the precursor to everything material.

Consciousness, I therefore believe, is everything *as it is*. Consciousness and God are one-and-the-same, and the known universe is God's mechanism for experiencing Itself. Consciousness is the Source of all matter, it is the Monad, the Absolute, it is Universal Love, the Tao, and the ultimate unchanging reality Brahman. As in Neoplatonism, everything is derived from The One. From absolute simplicity (Consciousness), emerges arbitrary and progressive complexity (the known universe). When matter manifests from Consciousness, the One becomes two, and matter encompasses all dualities (yin and yang). Nothing can exist without its interconnected counterpart.

Yin and yang are like a wave of energy; the up cannot exist without the down, which is how life is, and why acceptance of the 'downs' as well as the 'ups' is the key to contentment. Love cannot exist without fear, light cannot exist without darkness, male cannot exist without female, and saints cannot exist without psychopaths. This is very important because if you are not accepting of *what is*, you will never have peace of mind, as you will be forever fighting against reality and labelling people and events 'positive' or 'negative.' This is a cognitive trap that creates mental discomfort, emotional dis-ease, or a general underlying dissatisfaction (The Spiritual Malady). Acceptance of *what is*, therefore, is the key to peace of mind and contentment. If you have no preferences, life will flow with ease.

It is written in Psalms 46:10 in the Old Testament of the *Holy Bible* (King James version), "Be still and know that I am God," which I believe means, no matter how chaotic and crazy your mind and your emotions may be, when you are completely still and silent, you can experience God (Consciousness) within, which, unlike your physical body, is eternal and never changes. If you are to believe that Consciousness is everything manifesting at different frequencies of energy, you must understand it and experience it for yourself. You mustn't take my word for it, nor simply intellectualize it, as this theory can be easily rejected on face value because your ego-mind will disagree, as your ego-mind survives on the concept of dualism (separation from Source). However, if you accept Monism (oneness), first through understanding, then direct experience through meditation and mindfulness, you will fully accept that your physical body is nothing more than a vessel for Consciousness (God) to work through, and that 'You' as an entity, separate from Consciousness, is merely an illusion created by your ego-mind. Paradoxically, your ego-mind is also a manifestation of Consciousness vibrating at a "grosser" energy frequency, as our teacher, S.N Goenka, termed it on the retreat.

Mahayana Buddhism defines 'The Eight Consciousnesses' as: the five sense consciousnesses (sight, hearing, taste, smell, touch) plus the 'mental consciousness,' the 'defiled mental consciousness,' and the 'fundamental store-house consciousness,' which is the basis of the other seven. I consider the ego to be the 'defiled mental consciousness,' which is the part of your identity that you consider to be your 'self,' separate from others. The ego is strengthened by identification with the physical body and is comprised of involuntary thought patterns that often take the shape of a storyline in which 'You' are the main character. It is a fundamentally selfish entity that develops when every child is approximately two years of age and is driven by desire (craving). The ego is also the main obstruction to self-actualization/Enlightenment. The stronger your ego-construct, or sense of self, the more it separates you from others and simultaneously creates low self-esteem due to comparison. If you find yourself comparing yourself to other people and concluding you are either 'better' or 'worse' than them, this is your ego at play.

The 'mental consciousness,' which is responsible for perception of the external world, problem solving, control of motor functions, adaptation to situations, regulation of distress, reconciliation of conflicting impulses, and memory, works in tandem with the ego to help you function with an identity in the world. This is why I use the term ego-mind to describe these combined aspects of Consciousness. If your ego-mind was completely wiped and your memory lost, you would be aware only of the impersonal 'I am,' which is the fundamental store-house consciousness.

Whereas I do not differentiate between Consciousness and Soul (I imagine each Soul as a unique spark of Consciousness from the divine flame of Spirit), Buddhism does not recognize the existence of an eternal, essential, and absolute something called a Soul, or self, at the core of all human beings and living creatures. It recognizes only the emergence of the ever-decaying body, and the ever-changing ego-mind, which essentially inhabits and controls your body like an alien life-form. The more you 'buy-in' to your ego-mind-chatter, the more unmanageable your life can become, as your ego-mind can be like a washing machine constantly set to 'spin.' This can become increasingly stressful and very difficult for you to slow down and relax with a 'washing machine head.' To gain peace, one must practice disassociating from the ego-mind (and its inherent selfishness and separateness) by expanding awareness of your true nature (Consciousness) through meditation and mindfulness, or other spiritual practices, such as mantras or yoga.

The illusion of separateness (I am Ren, she is Adele) created by the ego-mind, is necessary for every sentient being to function in the world with 'free-will,' so we can make choices. However, upon careful investigation, I've found that free-will is actually an illusion because, although we are always free to decide what actions to take in any given moment, we never have any control over the outcome of our actions. All the choices we make are based on our environmental conditioning and our genes, which are pre-determined by Consciousness. Science tells us that genetics pre-determine what you have the capacity to become, and every action you take is predetermined by the subconscious mind (fundamental store-house consciousness), as the brain 'registers' the decision to make a movement *before* you consciously decide to move. Pioneering scientist in the field of human consciousness, Benjamin Libet, discovered that an electrical potential (of just a few microvolts) is visible in the brain long before the subject flexes a finger. Libet's experiments in the 1980's seemed to show evidence for a lack of free-will in human subjects, and the question still remains, what is the source of that electrical charge in the brain?

Albert Einstein, Ramesh Balsekar, and the great Indian sage Ramana Maharshi shared a belief in the philosophy of Determinism; that everything is predetermined by forces over which we have no control. Free-will is essentially an illusion because it is based on just two factors: one's genes and one's conditioning – and we have no control over either. For example, I was born a male, in Manchester (UK) and given a name by my parents. I didn't ask to be male, or to be given my name, or to be born to my particular mother and father. I had no choice in the matter and I've never had any control over the conditioning/programming I received at home, at school, or in society, and I've never had any control over the outcomes of my actions either. It is all a matter of fate, and what is fate but the will of a Higher Power?

As a consequence of our actions, we either get what we desire, we don't get what we desire, or we get something totally unexpected (sometimes better than we expected and sometimes worse), but whatever happens is never in our control. For example, I made the decision to drink alcohol when I was twelve years of age but I didn't choose to be an alcoholic, and I didn't choose to 'get' recovery from alcoholism – this was unexpected and better than I could have ever imagined. "We all dance to a mysterious tune intoned in the distance by an invisible piper," according to Einstein. This begs the question to which we definitely do not yet have a definitive answer: is everything that happens already written, and if so, who, or what, writes it?

In theosophy (an esoteric religious movement established in the United States during the late 19th Century) and anthroposophy (a philosophy founded by esotericist Rudolf Steiner following his exclusion from the Theosophical Society), the 'Akashic Records' are believed to be a compendium of the thoughts, words, and deeds of all living creatures ever to have occurred in the past, present, or future. They are said to be viewed like an immense photographic film encoded in a non-physical but intellectually comprehensible spiritual realm of astral light (known as the etheric plane) existing beyond the range of human senses, reputedly accessible through meditation. Akasha is a Sanskrit word translating to 'Primary substance,' and according to *The Aquarian Gospel of Jesus the Christ*, authored by American preacher Levi H. Dowling (who reportedly used the Akashic Records as the source of his information), Jesus Christ said, "It is the first stage in the crystallization of spirit... that is of exquisite fineness and is so sensitive that the slightest vibration of ether registers an indelible impression on it."

According to Dowling, Jesus also stated that, "all primordial substance is spirit moving at lower rates of vibration, becoming a coagulum... It is everywhere present. It is in very fact the 'Universal Mind' of which our metaphysicians speak." Jesus goes on to explain that there are three phases of Consciousness:
1 – Consciousness of the omnipotence of God and man.
2 – Consciousness of Divine Love (or Christ Consciousness).
3 – Consciousness of the Holy Breath (or Supreme Intelligence), and that these phases of Consciousness do not necessarily imply either of the others. A person can be filled with the Divine Love of God, for example, and far advanced in the science of Christ Consciousness yet completely ignorant of the laws of nature and spiritual things – therefore not in rapport with the Holy Breath. When the mind of man is in exact accord with the Universal Mind (or Holy Breath), man enters into a conscious recognition of the Akashic impressions, and he may collect them and translate them into any language. Those who perceive these record-books of

God, such as Levi H. Dowling and Gautama Buddha when he reached Nirvana (ultimate liberation from suffering) and became Enlightened, see: the life experiences of every human being since time began, the reactions to experience of the entire animal kingdom, and the aggregation of the thought-forms of karmic nature (based on desire/craving) of every human being throughout time.

The Akashic Records might simply be an intriguing metaphor to explain Enlightenment, however, I've had so many inexplicable spiritual, paranormal, and psychedelic experiences that I remain open-minded. Some of the most intelligent scientists of our age, including Donald D. Hoffman, who wrote, *The Case Against Reality: How Evolution Hid the Truth from Our Eyes*, are starting to consider that everything, including space-time, emerges from Consciousness (the Akasha). Following his Enlightenment, Gautama Buddha taught, "Two things are eternal, 'Akasha' and 'Nirvana.' Everything has come out of Akasha in obedience to a law of motion inherent in it, and, passes away. No-thing ever comes out of nothing."

Predetermination is more about challenging the ingrained and inaccurate belief that an individual has control of what's happening in their life, rather than proving that the full story has already been written. For me, control is definitely an illusion, and the magical unfolding of contemplations, synchronistic events (of which I have had an abundance of experience), realizations, and insights, which happen time and time again and are clearly outside of my doing – and are not possibly happening by accident – suggests proof of predetermination.

In September 2017, under the psychedelic influence of the Amazonian plant medicine ayahuasca, my ego-mind-interface switched off when my brain's default mode network went offline and my organic operating system received, interpreted, and disseminated a binary 'download' of universal source code. This ancient wisdom helped me realize that my ego-mind is essentially being driven around in an autonomous vehicle that it continuously keeps trying to take control of, when it would do better to simply allow the vehicle to continue on its predetermined course. This analogy is the best my limited intellect can do in attempting to make sense of concepts that are so complicated I don't think our ego-minds will ever be capable of fully comprehending the enormity. Intuitively I feel that one must transcend the ego-mind's intellect and reasoning in order to know 'Absolute Truth,' like Gautama Buddha did over 2500 years ago – before he ambiguously stated, "Events happen, deeds are done, but there is no individual doer of any deed."

This whole introduction might seem very esoteric, but it was essential to lay out the ostensibly mystical concepts of Consciousness, free-will, and a Higher Power in the most epistemological, simplistic, and scientific way possible – prior to talking about how to attain peace of mind and lasting happiness – because it is all inextricably linked in my opinion. My understanding of life has changed dramatically in the short space of time since publishing my third book, *Together: An Ayahausca Experience* in 2019. I can openly admit that I did what I think a lot of people do when writing about God in *Together*. Even though I mentioned the dark element of my trip and the hint of the demonic lurking in the darkness (which I consciously chose not to face), at the time, I did not accept the darkness as being just as much a part of God (and me) as light and love. It wasn't until my friend Barbarah introduced me to the teachings of Ramesh Balsekar that I understood and accepted that God is not only love, God is *all*. The laws of nature (including suffering under the banners of craving, aversion, and ignorance) were established millions of years before life evolved and therefore take precedence over all human affairs. Suffering is not 'bad,' it is simply part of life; the eb-and-flow of pleasure and pain. To quote one of my favorite bands, Vampire Weekend, "Pain is as natural as the rain."

Another major issue that must be addressed at this point is the word 'God,' as it is indivisible from religion and is always subject to anthropomorphization. Similarly, 'Consciousness' sounds like a 'thing' to me, so I refer to my own Higher Power as, 'The Organizing Principle' (T.O.P for short), which is an abstraction, sounding more like a code, formula, sequencer, or enigma. This makes sense to me because Consciousness organizes the physical universe and it is the principle truth that serves as the foundation for all matter and sentient life. Choosing to orient your life in line with "God's will," as Jesus referred to it, rather than the ignorance and incessant desires and aversions of your ego-mind is, therefore, my recommended way of facilitating the changes necessary to cultivate peace of mind and contentment. Once you've had time to consider the question, what is God for you? I invite you to define, and understand, your own conception of a Higher Power.

Progressive detachment from the desires, aversions, and ignorance of your ego-mind, and sharing a positive message of love and service through altruistic actions, are the goals I would urge you to aim for on your human journey. As I have experienced and witnessed numerous times with my family and friends, and the family and friends of my 'sponsees' (people who I 'sponsor' in Twelve Step fellowships), personal change can be so powerful that it can effect change in others – if they choose to follow your example. This is known as, 'the ripple effect.' Now is the time, therefore, to institute your own personal program of change for the betterment of humanity.

The following pages are a series of ten lessons that, once learned, might help you begin your recovery from obsessive and unmanageable thinking, and the underlying emotional disorder that we all suffer from in varying degrees. The aim of this book is simply to help you attain peace of mind and happiness, exponentially, which you will experience as a result of your evolution, should you choose to embark on a journey of change. As you incorporate these lessons, I hope you might come to notice how unmanageable your thoughts and emotions can be, which is experienced as an underlying dis-ease (bordering on despair at times). I also hope you might accept that Consciousness is your intuitive guide from deep within, that no human power or material satisfaction can relieve your dis-ease, and that a Higher Power (of your own understanding) can – once He/She/It is discovered.

**"PATIENCE IS BITTER,
BUT ITS FRUIT IS SWEET"**

– Aristotle (Greek philosopher during the
Classical period in Ancient Greece)

THE FIRST LESSON:
PATIENCE & TOLERANCE

Since beginning my journey of change in 2010 and writing my first book *Addiction Prevention: Twelve Steps To Spiritual Awakening* in 2015, I've learned some simple but very important lessons that I wish to share, which have helped me attain peace of mind and contentment. In the aforementioned book I confronted the addiction problem by offering a mainstream explanation of 'The Spiritual Malady' (represented by the three-spoke symbol on the cover of this book, which translates to the physical, psychological, and emotional human system, encompassed by the spiritual). The Spiritual Malady usually and initially manifests as impatience with, and intolerance of, other people. Striving for patience and tolerance is a spiritual pursuit that will set you on a path toward peace of mind and contentment because you will rarely be upset by the attitudes and behaviors of others. To get to this emotionally balanced place, first must come self-acceptance. This is achieved by dropping the 'ideal self' fantasy of who you think you are and who you wish to be, and replacing it with knowledge of your true self (Consciousness). If you can't accept yourself as you are, you'll never accept other people *as they are*. Much of what I have written in this book is about how to become accepting of yourself so you can accept other people. Acceptance is unconditional love but it is not the same as approval. You don't have to like a person or approve of their behavior to accept them.

Most people are not substance or behavioral addicts. Most people are recreational substance users (including alcohol) and/or recreational gamblers, shoppers, and exercisers, whose use or behavior ranges from moderate to heavy at varying times in their lives. This doesn't mean that moderate users or gamblers are not suffering from The Spiritual Malady, because everyone has their own pain, and drug use or pleasurable behaviors are a way of avoiding or masking that pain. I also explained in my first book how The Twelve Step Program could be universally applied to treat The Spiritual Malady in exactly the same way the Buddhist Eight-Fold Path can be universally applied to treat human suffering.

Addiction is a major health problem that costs the healthcare system as much as cancer and cardiovascular disorders, and all other mental illnesses combined (about £40 billion per year in 2010). At its core, addiction is a state of altered brain function, which leads to fundamental changes in behavior that manifest due to repeated use of substances, such as alcohol, heroin, cocaine, or sugar, or behaviors, such as gambling, exercise, shopping, or sex. The key feature of addiction is a state of habitual behavior that is initially enjoyable but eventually becomes habitual and (most often) no longer enjoyable due to adverse consequences. The urge to engage in the behavior becomes so powerful that it interferes with normal life, often to the point of overtaking work, personal relationships, and family activities. At this point the person can be said to be addicted, as the addict's every thought and action is directed to their behavior and/or substance misuse, and everything else in their life suffers as a result. If the addictive substance or behavior is not possible because they don't have enough money for example, then feelings of intense distress emerge, which can lead to dangerously impulsive and sometimes aggressive actions. In the case of drug addiction, the situation is compounded by the occurrence of withdrawal symptoms that cause further distress and motivate desperate attempts to find more of the substance. This urge to get the drug may be so overpowering that addicts will commit seemingly random crimes to get the resources to buy more drugs. Roughly 70% of all acquisitive crime in society is associated with drug use.

Addiction is driven by a complex set of internal and external factors. The external factors are well understood: the more access to the desired drug or behavior the more addiction there is. The internal factors have always been less clear. Addiction to gambling and other behaviors, such as sex or shopping, tells us that the brain can develop addictive urges independent of changing its chemistry with substances. All addictions share a common thread in that they are initially pleasurable activities, often extremely enjoyable, which results in these behaviors hijacking the brain's pleasure/reward system so that naturally enjoyable activities, such as family life or work, become devalued and the more excessive, addictive behaviors take control.

Not everyone who engages in drug use or gambling becomes addicted to them, so clearly other factors are important, but these are not yet fully understood by science. Some people may be particularly sensitive to the pleasurable effects of substances and/or behaviors because they come from deprived backgrounds, yet addiction may occur in others because of an inability to adopt coping strategies. Some people may have a genetic predisposition to develop compulsive behavior patterns, and some unfortunate people may have several of these vulnerability factors plus a genetic predisposition. Fundamentally, the simplest way to explain it is: addiction is all about escaping or avoiding *what is*. Presence (being in the moment), therefore, is the antidote to the constant desire to escape or avoid feelings, thoughts, or circumstances, but being present with your underlying and often unconscious pain is not that easy, which is why people continually fall back (relapse) into 'using' habits. If you don't deal with the underlying causes, the symptoms always come back.

A significant amount of recreational drug use is actually for self-medication purposes (either conscious or unconscious), with examples including cannabis for insomnia, alcohol to reduce anxiety, and opioids for pain relief. Therapeutic use can escalate into addiction for some people but not all, and there are many drugs that are used for medicinal purposes that are not addictive. Psychedelics, such as LSD, San Pedro, Peyote, ayahuasca, and psilocybin (magic mushrooms), are not toxic or addictive because they do not activate the brain's dopaminergic pathways in the same way as addictive drugs, such as nicotine, sugar, alcohol, heroin, crack-cocaine, methamphetamine (crystal meth), and Novel Psychoactive Substances (NPS). Some drugs have a much lower risk of addiction, such as MDMA/Ecstasy because it only partially excites the brain's dopamine receptors. Starting to use drugs may initially be a lifestyle choice but once a person has 'crossed the line' and addiction sets in, choosing to stop without help is much more difficult – if not impossible – for most people.

We are only just beginning to understand how addictions form. The pleasurable/rewarding effects of substances and behaviors are mediated in the brain through the release of chemicals, such as dopamine by cocaine, amphetamines, and nicotine, endorphins by heroin, and both by alcohol. The pleasures/rewards are then laid down as deep-seated memories through changes in other neurotransmitters, which then link the location and experiences of the addiction with the emotional effects. These are often the most powerfully positive ones the addict has ever experienced, which explains why addicts are so driven to experience them again and again. This was certainly my experience of using Ecstasy for the first time, which I often describe as a synthesized spiritual experience of immense love. When these types of memories re-occur, they are experienced as cravings, which demand cessation, and can be so strong and so urgent that they can lead an abstinent addict, who doesn't have any coping strategies in place, to relapse.

A great deal of research has been conducted into the role of dopamine in addiction. We now know that low dopamine and high opioid receptor levels in the brain predict drug use and craving, and that addiction is not a 'lifestyle choice.' It's a serious, often lethal disease caused by an enduring (possibly permanent) change in brain function – whereby an excessive response to stimulation from substances and behaviors by the brain's dopamine receptors moves into other areas of the brain – where habit patterns are formed. This shift from voluntary to involuntary (habitual) explains a common complaint of addicts who don't want to continue their addiction but can't stop. Addiction can therefore be understood as a loss of control over what starts out as a voluntary behavior, which is exactly how I experienced my alcoholism.

For some addictions, especially heroin, the risk to the addict (life expectancy less than that from many cancers) and to society (from crime and infectious diseases such as Hep-C and HIV), is so high that the prescription of substitute medications (methadone and buprenorphine), or even heroin itself in some countries, saves lives and reduces crime. As well as reducing crime and social costs by removing the need for addicts to commit offences to feed their habit, they also protect addicts from accidental overdose and reduce risk of infections – mainly from sharing needles and sexual intercourse. Similar substitute pharmacological approaches exist for other addictions, such as Alcover and baclofen for alcohol addiction, but I don't believe the addict begins to recover, from what is essentially a hopeless condition of body and mind, until they address The Spiritual Malady at the root of their addiction.

I believe addiction can be simplified to three stages: the last stage is physical dependence on a substance or behavior, the second stage is the mental obsession or insanity of the mind just before using a substance or acting-out a behavior (knowing what the consequences of 'using' or 'acting out' might be), and the first stage is The Spiritual Malady; the inward condition that triggers the second stage. Symptoms of The Spiritual Malady, as described in the 'Big book,' *Alcoholics Anonymous: The Story of How Many Thousands of Men and Women Have Recovered from Alcoholism*, are as follows:

- Being restless, irritable, and discontented
- Having trouble with personal relationships
- Not being able to control our emotional natures
- Being a prey to (or suffering from) misery and depression
- Not being able to make a living (or a happy and successful life)
- Having feelings of uselessness
- Being full of fear
- Unhappiness
- The inability to be of real help to other people
- Being like the actor who wants to run the whole show
- Being driven by a hundred forms of fear, self-delusion, self-seeking, and self-pity
- Self-will run riot
- Leading a double life
- Living like a tornado running through the lives of others
- Exhibiting selfish and inconsiderate habits

Collectively, these symptoms are what we in Twelve Step fellowships refer to as the 'ism' (of alcoholism), which might be an acronym for, 'inner spiritual malady,' or 'I separate myself,' or 'it separates me.' The 'ism' is essentially the ego-mind; the driving force of which is explained in 'The Big Book' as, "Selfishness-self-centeredness." If this selfish-self-centeredness continues to manifest in the addict's life (including those who are not using drugs and still going to Twelve Step meetings), and the ego-mind's demands are not continually addressed and questioned by daily application of The Steps, the abstinent addict is very likely to use drugs again eventually – or continue to live miserably in isolation with symptoms of The Spiritual Malady. This is the reason why many thousands of men and women are suffering with emotional and mental health issues and addictions, and why some addicts – with many years of abstinence but no formal program – find themselves in psychiatric hospitals, or commit suicide. This is also why, after a period of sobriety, some addicts return to their drug of choice even when they don't want to. Addressing The Spiritual Malady as the root cause of both addiction and general unhappiness is therefore of paramount importance!

Addiction is defined as a chronic, relapsing disorder characterized by compulsive substance misuse and/or behavior seeking, continued use/practice of substances/behaviors despite harmful consequences, and long-lasting changes in the brain. Although chronic addicts have less impulse control than 'non-addicts' (which gets progressively worse in active addiction), and the 'reward system' in the brain of a chronic addict is likely hyper-sensitive, and the brain of a chronic addict is less attuned to withdrawal (making withdrawal much less tolerable), I firmly believe that substance and/or behavioral addiction is primarily an emotional disorder that manifests as mental health and physical health issues. I also believe that anyone is susceptible to addiction, which is exacerbated by our contemporary, consumer-driven culture, as we eat too much, drink too much, buy too much, and generally desire too much. The worship of money, power, status, celebrity, entertainment, and brands – in the form of consumerism – has essentially become the religion of addiction, as people tend to confuse material and synthesized pleasures with true happiness. Whereas pleasure is a feeling we get from experiences, happiness is contentment despite experiences – whether they are pleasurable or not.

Our desire (craving) for more, which materializes on the physical plane in the brain's dopamine reward system as a sense of something 'lacking,' is the source of all our emotional suffering; the fruitless mission to fill the (sometimes gaping) hole inside us with an endless range of pleasures and material satisfactions that all our senses constantly cry-out for. This 'hole in our soul' *is* The Spiritual Malady and I believe everyone suffers from it in varying degrees, as we all consume more and more things, believing we are hungry for more food, more drugs, more status, more thrills, more money, or more possessions, when we are in fact hungry for connection; not only connection with each other but connection with something greater that is actually deep down within all of us. This is why addiction is considered a 'disease of more' in Twelve Step fellowships, and the solution prescribed is: abstinence from the substance/behavior of choice and connection with a Higher Power (of your own understanding).

I personally identify as an alcoholic, someone who has lost the ability to control my drinking once I take the first alcoholic drink, and someone to whom alcohol is a poison that once consumed causes nothing but physical, psychological, emotional, and social damage in my life. I haven't tested whether this is still the case since September 2009, but I believe it to be so, as I could never drink alcohol safely before I got sober. I believe my disease (The Spiritual Malady), that I was attempting to medicate with alcohol, has only been arrested, not cured. I also believe I will always be physically intolerant to alcohol no matter how psychologically or emotionally 'well' I become in the future, as my malleable brain has been changed and impaired by misuse of the substance over a ten-year period.

I also identify as an addict because at one stage or another, I've lost my ability to control my intake of certain drugs including Ecstasy, cocaine, caffeine, and sugar, and behaviors such as exercise, shopping, work, and sex. Using substances and acting out behaviors is something that I often do, even though I don't want to, against my own will; a mental obsession beyond my control. Yet when I work a Twelve Step Program (on any given addiction) it keeps my addiction at bay. Although I have occasional lapses – usually with sugar, shopping, and exercise, I've progressively gained more choice over the way I use substances and over the behaviors I perform. I put this down to following the suggestions of The Twelve Step Program – with specific emphasis on Step Ten (taking daily moral inventory), Step Eleven (prayer and meditation to improve my conscious contact with a Higher Power of my own understanding), and Step Twelve (passing on the message to those still suffering with addiction).

Meditation and prayer, I believe, has been the keystone to arresting my emotional dis-ease and gaining choice over my obsessive-compulsive thoughts that manifest as physical addictions. This is because meditation evolves the brain's processing center (the amygdala), which is highly involved with different emotional responses, impulsive behaviors, and 'fight, flight, or freeze' fear responses. By surrendering to my powerlessness over certain substances and behaviors, I paradoxically gain the power of choice not to 'use' or 'act out,' rather than constantly being driven by a compulsion beyond my control. My level of surrender perfectly coincides with my level of abstinence; absolute surrender equals absolute abstinence, one day at a time. When I pray and ask for a sober day, my ego is formally surrendering to Consciousness. When I surrender my will (my desires, my aversions, and my ignorance), and 'turn it over' to my Higher Power (by saying, "Thy will be done"), I am no longer battling with my Higher Power and peace *from* my ego-mind is attained.

To learn to make the right choices in life, I believe you have to get in touch with that ineffable part of you that knows what's right for you, so you can make decisions from intuition (Consciousness) rather than from reason. To achieve this, you'll need to experience periods of solitude – if only thirty minutes per day. People can be afraid of solitude because they can hear all sorts of uncomfortable truths in the silence and receive solutions to their problems, but they might not be ready and willing to take the action required. They avoid solitude, because it can be initially uncomfortable, in the same way we avoid other things that might be good for us, such as moderate exercise, reading books, or eating healthily. On the Vipassana retreat, in the solitude of ten days silent meditation, there was an amplification of every participants internal ego-mind-chatter, which some people couldn't handle, so they left the retreat rather than sit with it. My mind, for example, initially created elaborate fantasies about some of the participants on the retreat, which turned out to be completely false once the silence was lifted and I had chance to speak with the individuals concerned.

Thanks to a general preoccupation with fantasy, working, sleeping, eating, and going places to be entertained, plus a general fear of solitude, most people rarely analyze themselves. By evading self-analysis, however, you'll never know true peace of mind and lasting happiness, and you'll never know why you're always seeking something *more*. You'll just carry on binging on dopamine-enhancing substances and behaviors that give you a 'quick fix,' as I did for many years. As a self-aware addict in recovery, I recognize the part of me, which takes over when I'm in 'addiction mode,' fixing on whatever I'm fixing on (usually chocolate these days), that wants to destroy itself. When recovering addicts say, "My addict wants me dead," I imagine it would sound extreme, ludicrous even, to the 'non-addict,' but to the active addict and recovering addict (especially those who have experienced intrusive thoughts), we can strongly relate. The super-charged ego-mind of the addict craves oblivion to switch off from the feelings that feed it. All it wants is peace, and there is nothing more peaceful than death. This is why suicide becomes an option if The Spiritual Malady is not treated.

Self-analysis through prayer, meditation, and taking 'moral inventory,' is the greatest method to affect change and attain emotional balance and peace of mind, as it helps you de-code and re-program yourself toward a more peaceful cognitive orientation. You then become less prone to obsessive-compulsive behavior binges. Regarding the question of emotional sobriety, Alcoholics Anonymous Co-founder Bill Wilson said, "I think that many old-sters who have put our A.A 'booze cure' to severe but successful tests still find they often lack emotional sobriety. Perhaps they will be the spearhead for the next major development in A.A – the development of much more real maturity and balance (which is to say, humility) in our relations with ourselves, with our fellows, and with God."

In September 2018, having just finished a ten-day Vipassana silent meditation retreat at Dhamma Dipa in Hereford, UK, living like a monk by waking up at 4am, spending more-or-less every waking moment in silence, eating only two vegetarian meals per day, meditating for a minimum of eight hours per day (including three hours in solitude), and going to bed at 9.30pm, I was slightly disappointed not to be fully 'Enlightened' following so much self-analysis! However, it was one of the most transformational and life changing experiences of my life, and it cemented certain lessons that comprise much of this book. I hope these lessons help you to overcome your own suffering by freeing you from the bondage of your selfish, self-centered thought processes, and help you attain peace of mind, as I strongly believe that contentment and therefore lasting happiness cannot be experienced without it.

On 'day 0,' before the course began, Lawrie (an 'old student' who was on retreat for the 5th time) explained to me that, whereas drinking the psychedelic plant medicine ayahuasca (which I drank the previous January) was like flying to the top of a mountain in a helicopter to the destination marked 'Enlightenment,' Vipassana is like climbing to the top of the mountain very slowly, but the emptiness and spaciousness of Enlightenment is still the same.

I would embellish his analogy thus: my ayahuasca experience was like being flown to the top of a mountain with a small group of people in a helicopter through turbulent skies, driven by an invisible woman who taught me lessons as we flew. Along the journey, I was sick in a bucket a few times and I wanted to jump off the helicopter at points but we eventually came through the turbulence and emerged at the summit – where my pilot ('Mother Ayahuasca') set me down on the blissful peak of Enlightenment and I stayed there for a few hours. Vipassana meditation, on the other hand, was like climbing up the mountain with a large group of people, to whom I couldn't speak (due to a vow of noble silence). We climbed for five days through rough terrain and weather, and when we reached the summit of Enlightenment, it was blissful, but we had to come down after a few moments.

As a result of no formal integration following the ayahuasca ceremony due to complications that put the ceremony back twelve hours, when it was time to come down from my ayahuasca journey I felt shaky and unsure how to navigate, but when I came down from my Vipassana journey we all knew the way down and we all had the knowledge for future reference of how to scale and descend the mountainous ranges and rough terrains of deep meditation.

Following the retreat, I could see how, in the past, when I was addictively behaving and using substances, I was trying to reach the top of the mountain as quickly as possible. It was all about the destination and had nothing to do with experiencing the journey. I also had zero patience back then to even attempt the journey and I always wanted a short-cut to the top of the mountain. Patience, I noted during the retreat, is an essential pre-requisite to peace of mind. If you're going to strive for peace of mind and lasting happiness, you're going to need bags of patience.

A few months after the retreat I was discussing my Vipassana experience versus my ayahuasca experience with my friend Carl, who introduced me to these wise words from the late British-American philosopher Alan Watts: "Psychedelic experience is only a glimpse of genuine mystical insight, but a glimpse which can be matured and deepened by the various ways of meditation in which drugs are no longer necessary or useful. If you get the message, hang up the phone. For psychedelic drugs are simply instruments, like microscopes, telescopes, and telephones. The biologist does not sit with his eye permanently glued to the microscope, he goes away and works on what he has seen."

I explained to Carl that one psychedelic experience wasn't quite enough for me to get the message, and not long after (in October 2019), I had another revelatory psychedelic experience with psilocybin (magic) mushrooms in the dramatic woodlands and stark moorland plateaus of the Peak District National Park in central England.

Bill-Wilson-inspired psychedelic therapy became part of my recovery journey in September 2017 at the aforementioned ayahuasca retreat in Mallorca, where I met my brother-from-another-mother Luke. The word psychedelic essentially means 'revealing what is hidden,' which is why the use of psychedelics, in the appropriate set and setting, is a potent form of psychotherapy, as they reveal the symptoms of illnesses buried deep in our subconscious. It takes time and patience to adapt, change, or dissolve rigid belief systems, and I had to do three years of research on psychedelics before I came to the conclusion, similarly to Alcoholics Anonymous Co-founder Bill Wilson, who began experimenting with LSD in 1956, that without the experience of psychedelics I would never know with any certainty that *everything is interconnected by Consciousness.* "The sensation that the partition between 'here' and 'there' has become very thin is constantly with me," said Wilson following his first LSD 'trip.' Wilson was so convinced that LSD could help alcoholics by chemically inducing a spiritual awakening and curing their depression that he even introduced one of his sponsees, Tom Powers (who co-wrote *The Twelve Steps and Twelve Traditions)*, to LSD.

Going against the advice of my peers in Twelve Step fellowships, I made the decision to 'journey' with ayahuasca in 2017 to understand if the medicine could help addicts overcome emotional and mental health issues at the root of their addictions and have a spiritual experience that might introduce them to a Higher Power, so they could work through The Twelve Step Program without any prejudice toward the word 'God,' which puts off many people. In an email to my friend John (before his first ayahuasca ceremony in 2010), renowned addiction and trauma specialist, Dr. Gabor Maté, wrote, "I understand the A.A suspicion of 'drugs.' But ayahuasca is not a drug anyone uses for recreational purposes. Unlike addicted drug use, the purpose of which is to lower one's level of consciousness and awareness, ayahuasca, used in the proper context with the right leadership, gives access to higher awareness. It does not encourage ongoing use."

My experience with ayahuasca was life-changingly therapeutic and analogous to ten years of psychotherapy in one eight-hour session. Thanks to my research, I knew that success (in the sense of processing my trauma and healing from it) hinged on integration after the ceremony, and my intentions before the ceremony, which were: to figure out if Adele and I were meant to be together; to drop selfishness; to become more open and honest in my relationships; and to meet God. Thankfully, I did meet my Higher Power, Adele and I are now engaged with a baby daughter, I am rarely selfish these days, and I am far more open and honest in my relationships. My experience with psilocybin was the final part of my integration of these lessons, as everything clicked into place.

Although any drug can be used as a means of escape (including psychedelics), mushrooms and other plant medicines are not addictive, and when used in the appropriate set (mindset) and setting (the conditions under which you 'trip') they can have hugely therapeutic benefits. Two years after my ayahuasca experience, I was offered, and took, the opportunity to journey with psilocybin (magic) mushrooms for the first time, which helped me figure out some more relationship issues and affirmed to me that Consciousness pervades everything. My intention was to heal and grow while immersed in nature alongside Luke, whom I felt safe with because he is a seasoned 'psychonaut' (someone who explores altered states of consciousness, especially through the use of psychedelics).

One cloudy Autumn day in October 2019, Luke drove us both – in his mint-green VW van – to a beautiful spot on a hill in the Peak District overlooking a thick forest in a deep valley with a backdrop of rolling emerald and chestnut hills. We sat in the back of the van and got dressed into our hiking gear before we ate approximately 15 grams of fresh psilocybin mushrooms mixed with a handful of cashew nuts to mask the earthy taste and make them more palatable.

We set off rambling down-hill through lush fields into the woods where the lines of trees got denser, as we waded through undergrowth that got thicker and thicker and evermore exotic-looking. I imagined it was how it might be if we'd been air-lifted into the Amazon basin like British former SAS serviceman and survival instructor Bear Grylls, and I simultaneously felt excitement and trepidation as I acknowledged the mushrooms had begun to take effect. My vision was becoming hazy and I was feeling a little nauseous, which Luke assured me was standard fare.

Luke found a clearing in the woods and we sat down on the grass. The medicine had strongly taken hold of both of us by this point and we joked around a bit before our laughter turned into hysterics bordering on lunacy, as we surrendered to the medicine. Luke's laugh was impish and even his face had taken on a mischievous, almost gremlinesque character. I highlighted his cackle and Luke said his girlfriend Kate had noted the same impishness when she had 'tripped' with him in the past. It seemed we were simply laughing at laughing itself and the big message I received from this was to be joyful at every opportunity. Every time I closed my eyes, intense, colorful psychedelic fractals exploding in front of my iris – and geometric patterns swirled around my eyelids. When I opened my eyes my world-view had transitioned from analogue to Super-HD. The trees seemed to be watching me enthused with kindness, their bark shimmering. I knew the psilocybin would access parts of my subconscious that are normally blocked from my conscious-awareness, and in that exposed and vulnerable state, I could face them, accept them, and ultimately move beyond them.

Fear struck me that I was getting 'off my head,' like I used to on drugs in clubs. I had a vivid flashback of being 'wrecked' in a nightclub, but I felt the compassionate spiritual presence of the forest and simultaneously a massive wave of assurance washed over me that this was definitely not the same; this was healing. I let out a groan and cried a little, which released the guilt and shame that I didn't even know my body had stored for over fifteen years. As I let go, I felt the guilt and shame of past actions related to my addiction leave my body – passing down my legs and out of my toes – absorbed by the moss beneath my feet. I let out a big sigh and I profoundly understood the Buddhist notion that 'clinging' (attachment) to anything (including the past) is the root cause of my suffering.

I lay on my back in the grass and looked up at the sky that appeared pixelated, which gave me the sense that we are living inside a program (or simulation) with everything mechanically doing its part. This reminded me that there are grand, mysterious forces – way beyond our limited understanding. Every time I breathed deeply the sky and the whole forest breathed with me, in-and-out, pulsating with the rhythm of my breath. The notion came to me that Consciousness is analogous to the sky, and clouds are like thoughts; some are beautiful and some are stormy. Clouds always pass and sky always remains; pure and free. If Consciousness is the Universal Mind/Source/the Akasha, and thoughts manifests from Consciousness, then mind must be shared, as all thoughts and ideas come from the same place. Luke smiled at me knowingly then commented that we are totally one with nature, which I acknowledged and agreed with, but somehow I still felt separated. In hindsight, I think it was because I wasn't that used to being in nature, having rarely immersed myself in a forest before – It felt an almost alien environment. As a species, we have severed our connection from nature with technological advancement and that is why we feel separate, isolated, and sometimes completely alone. In fact, part of our dis-ease (the human condition), is that we think we are separate from nature, when we are in fact part of nature.

We decided to get up, shake off the loose energy (as we were both feeling a bit sedated) and keep moving deeper into the forest. As I walked, the power of the medicine intensified and my vision transitioned from Super-HD to 7-D Holographic. Luke stopped in a clearing about twenty yards ahead and we stood separately in awe and wonder at the spectacular forest, which was Avatar-esque – like the alien world of Pandora. The life-force of the forest – every plant, grass, moss, and tree – was luminous and translucent, of a beauty that stunned us both into silent rapture. We stood motionless for at least ten minutes, perfectly serene in psychedelic paradise with Mother Nature. I experienced no 'mental chatter,' just presence and peace, which, as we started walking again, gifted me a realization that Nature is to be worshipped and served, not to be used and abused.

Luke pre-warned me that we were about to walk through a pheasant-hunting ground, which alarmed me slightly, as I didn't want to bump into anyone who was not in the same psychedelic state as us. I was feeling wonderful as we walked into a clearing and past what we presumed to be pheasant traps, which felt a bit weird due to the connotation of nature-death. As I surveyed the landscape, I continued with the fantasy that we had landed on an alien world and we were walking into a trap. All of a sudden I heard a voice in the distance, "Excuse me, excuse me, where are you going? You're on private land."

As I turned around, what looked like an angry little computer game gremlin was marching at pace toward us with a tangible vibe of aggression. The little angry gremlin-like man, dressed in sage hunting garb, arrived in our vicinity and asked us where we were heading. Luke explained that we were simply rambling in no particular direction and the man proceeded to enlighten us that we categorically could not go the way we were heading because, "There's nothing down there!" This struck me as an odd comment, as there was nothing but trees in all directions. We weren't sure what the man's problem was, but he clearly wanted us off his land, and directed us back up a hill – close to the direction we'd just come from. Neither of us wanted to cause a scene, so we casually apologized for any inconvenience and headed up the hill along a dirt track. I noted the anger that the man had displayed was totally fear-based and it was certainly a lesson for me about tolerating a person's fear and anger without succumbing to my own. I also felt glad I am no longer trapped in that kind of aggressive personal ego-prison.

Needless to say, the encounter with the gremlin knocked me out of my serenity-state and into somewhat of a darker place. The hill was really steep and quite difficult to traverse due to lots of large rocks, and the further up the track we went the sparser the trees got, which made me feel exposed. As we shuffled closer to the top of the hill, all the trees were broken down and dead. It looked like an Armageddon scene and reminded me of the current decimation of the Amazon rain forest, which depressed me. We moved off the rocky track to our left – into the tree-graveyard – but I told Luke I wanted to be back in a happy place in the forest. Luke tripped over on a tree stump and seemed completely disoriented. He wanted to get to the brow of the hill to figure out where we were in relation to the van. He stopped and checked the time on his phone; we'd been tripping for around three hours and Luke felt we had at least another two-to-three hours left on our psychedelic journey.

We switched directions and headed back to the dirt track, which ended abruptly. We were back in the tree-graveyard but closer to the top of the hill. We stopped for a drink of water and a chat – sat on dead tree stumps – devoid of any life force. The *impermanence of everything* hit me hard. I pondered how important it is that we look after our planet; our life-giver. As I contemplated the end of the world, I felt simultaneously lost, empty, and despondent. My ego-mind wanted to avoid the feeling of despair but I sat with it for a few moments, sensing this 'dark night of the soul' experience would help me understand the importance of tolerating my emotions, which it did. Eventually, the melancholy lifted and I gazed at the beauty of the shimmering emerald and juniper hillside – roofed by undulating skies – and a feeling of contentment returned.

After we'd refreshed and pulled ourselves together, I suggested we walk over to an antiquated stone wall that was fifty yards to our right, then walk to the brow of the hill. As we climbed over the wall Luke laughed and proclaimed, "We're back where we started!" It was a huge relief, as I at once felt safe in the knowledge we were not lost and that 'home' was close by. We sat on the grassy ridge enjoying the antediluvian scenery – the hills rolling like waves on a vast ocean – discussing the importance of honesty. Adele was yet to know I had been on a vision quest in the woods, and I knew she wouldn't be best pleased that I hadn't told her. I explained to Luke that I often withhold the truth until after an event because I associate telling the truth with being told "no" by my parents when I was a teenager. I admitted that this behavior is clearly immature, dishonest, and inconsiderate, and I vowed to change.

The medicine was wearing off as we strolled across the peak of the hill toward the van, continuing our deep and meaningful conversation about how we both wanted to stop needing to be the 'man of the house,' respected, and 'in charge' at home. I explained my theory to Luke (which came to me following my ayahuasca experience), that God is the masculine seed of the universe but It cannot manifest without the divine feminine; therefore Mother is really the one in charge. Hindus believe that Shakti is both responsible for creation and the agent of all change. She is the personification of divine feminine creative power, sometimes referred to as, 'The Great Divine Mother.' Shakti is cosmic existence as well as liberation; Her most significant and powerful form being a mysterious psychospiritual force known as Kali, who is the destroyer of evil forces. Kali is said to destroy everything in you that is keeping you from God. Luke noted how it is definitely a female presence that emerges under the influence of ayahuasca, and I noted that 'Mother Aya' spoke directly to me, guiding me through my journey and scorched away my ego, so I could experience Oneness with my Higher Power. "We just need to trust our women more and be of service to them," I said. Luke then concluded, as we knelt on the grass marveling at mushrooms that glowed like tiny orange lightbulbs, we should worship our women like we should worship nature, and it is, "OK to be a servant..." That was the biggest truth bomb of all. We sat in silent contemplation on the verdant grass for a few moments.

I imagine anyone who has taken a big enough dose of psilocybin would report that Consciousness – in the psychedelic state – shows and tells you things you would not normally have the courage to see, hear, or admit to. About a hundred yards from his van, Luke tearfully shared some shameful past behavior with me that had come up for him – of which I could relate and empathize – before we thanked each other for the experience with a big hug. I had no idea it was going to be such a protracted and profound excursion. I think I was expecting two-to-three hours of mild psychedelia with interesting and insightful conversations – similar to how Bill Wilson had described his LSD experiences. It was so much more, and yet again (as I had previously experienced with ayahuasca), I felt that I had evolved slightly thanks to the medicine.

I don't believe ayahuasca or psilocybin heal you per se, I believe they dissolve your ego-mind's defenses and allow you to process emotions, which is immensely cathartic. I would not suggest the use of psychedelics unless you have exhausted all other options for somatic healing, as they are very powerful medicines that are best not used unless under the guidance of an experienced shaman – especially if it's your first time. However, if you want to continue changing, you often have to step outside your comfort zone and challenge yourself. In the same way that someone takes a spiritual pilgrimage, I ingested the 'magic' mushrooms in an attempt to better understand my own consciousness – and its interconnection with nature. In doing so, I faced my fears, which often requires a challenging voyage into the unknown, and cemented my understanding of impermanence; that all things arise and pass. To live in harmony with this great truth brings happiness.

“DEATH IS NOT THE OPPOSITE OF LIFE,
BUT A PART OF IT”

– Haruki Murakami (Japanese bestselling author)

LESSON TWO: IMPERMENANCE

On 'day 4' of the retreat, I was sat basking in glorious sunshine on a peanut colored bench by the side of an open, lush, grassy field when a one-inch brown fly with little red bug-eyes landed on my turquoise jacket – grabbing my attention. I inspected the fly mindfully, with a new-found equanimity, as my eyes had become like magnifying glasses due to intense periods of meditation. The realization dawned on me that the fly had just as much right to be there as I did. I contemplated how every fly, every spider, every insect, every animal, every plant, has just as much right to be here now on this planet as me. My ego had been deflated enough to understand this at a profound level.

My mind was catapulted away from the present moment – back two weeks earlier – to when I'd smashed a four-inch spider to death with a wooden stick, simply for spinning it's disgusting and unwanted thick grey web in the corner of my garage. I'd inspected the spider previously on a number of occasions prior to destroying it, and each time I'd considered killing it, my discreet inner voice (Consciousness) had told me not to do so. On that occasion, however, my aversion to spiders overcame me and I picked up a piece of wood that was resting against the garage wall, still knowing deep down that it was the wrong thing to do. The spider even got the sense something bad was about to happen, as it went into attack mode – lifting its front legs and bearing its pincers – which added fuel to my fiery rage. I swiftly smashed the wood into the spider three times and it fell to the floor dead, murdered. I didn't feel good. I hacked away the web, removing the evidence with my murder weapon, but the feeling of guilt remained. In that moment, I forgave myself for my ignorance. In retrospect, it was nothing more than an ego-fueled act of rage born out of fear.

All fears can be traced back to one ultimate fear, the ego's fear of death. Consciousness on the other hand can never fear death because it is eternal and never dies. Complete dis-identification with the ego resulting in self-actualization (Enlightenment) is, therefore, the end of fear. In the aforementioned instance, my fear of spiders led to resentment that led to anger, which led to the spider's death. This is the same process with all acts of anger, abuse, and violence. They all stem from fear, which is the greatest barrier to peace of mind and lasting happiness.

On 'day 5' of the retreat, sat on a different bench at the edge of the same field underneath the expansive azure sky, I calmly observed, with no fear at all, a two-inch black spider with orange markings trap a half-inch brown fly in its web – rolling it around until the fly apparently stopped breathing and its life-force drained away. The spider then retreated up its web, seemingly saving the fly for supper. I contemplated the impermanence of life, how it rises and falls like the breath, like physical sensations in the body – of which I was still acutely aware – pulsating through my hands and legs following a one-hour meditation.

I believe the idea of a Life-Force (the Élan Vital, as coined by French philosopher Henri Bergson), animating material form, was exorcised out of biology prematurely by reductionists in the early 1900's, who were quick to dismiss what they couldn't explain. To this day, we really don't know what makes a cell tick or how it works. It's like there's an invisible pianist playing the keys that move related to the music, but we don't know who (or what) is the Piano Player?

There comes a point in Vipassana meditation when you've focused your attention from one tiny part of your body to every part of your entire body – both outside and inside – and, if you are fortunate enough, you experience a quality of mind known as śamatha (in the Buddhist traditions), whereby your physical sense of self completely dissolves. All that remains is awareness of Consciousness, which is almost total liberation. It was during morning meditation on 'day 6' that I stopped clinging and my physical sense of 'self' dissolved slowly into the vibrations and sensations of atoms comprising my material form, before I became one with the Élan Vital. This was analogous to the ectoplasm that the caterpillar becomes inside the chrysalis when it's preparing to metamorphose into a butterfly. It was like I transitioned from being the light switch (with all its physical intricacies) to the electricity itself; Consciousness the current. Having focused down into one-pointed attention, I moved into Samadhi (equanimous and luminous mind), which was a timeless, ineffable place, similar to that which I experienced under the psychedelic influence of ayahuasca. I mustn't have been in Samadhi any more than a couple of minutes before awareness of my physical senses began to return and I was back in my body.

Call it Consciousness, call it Source, call it Love, God, Spirit, Élan Vital, the Tao, The Organizing Principle, the Piano Player, call is whatever you want; whatever *It* is, I have come to believe that *It* is all there is, and *It* is where everything begins and everything ends. It is the 'Oneness,' the Absolute, and it is the Power that comprises all matter. There is no death of the Life-Force, only a changing of energy states – from visible to invisible – in an eternal cycle; the wheel of Dharma (cosmic law and order). This experience was only a glimpse of Enlightenment but enough to help me understand the potential of Vipassana in helping one achieve absolute liberation from suffering.

By this point on the retreat I'd transcended 'normal' everyday mental and defiled consciousness and reached a place of deep knowing (store house consciousness), whereby I was able to knit together all the spiritual teachings I'd learned since 2009 into one snug fitting garment of wisdom. My step-daughter Isobel had asked me why I was going on a ten-day silent meditation retreat, as she couldn't understand why I wasn't going to be contactable for such a long period of time. I'd responded thoughtfully that it was to gain some insight and some calmness. She retorted, "I don't want you to be calm, I like you just the way you are!" Which sums it up really. We always feel like there's something to gain rather than being happy with ourselves and with things the way they are, and I was no different prior to the retreat. During my ten days of meditation, however, I progressively realized, and had consistently reinforced by the teachings of S.N Goenka, the notion that there's nothing to gain, or attain, and that I'm all I'll ever need to be as I am *right now*. Peace is all there is in the present moment and life, therefore, is perfect *as it is*. In other words, when you're Enlightened, pleasure and pain and fame and shame and loss and gain are all the same!

As I contemplated peace, I also came to the realization that it's best to face the fact that I, you, and everyone we love, are going to die. Prepare yourself for death immediately, don't put it off. The more you consider death the more comfortable with it you will be when it comes, and the more you will appreciate this precious life. Practice humble non-attachment, which is a state in which you overcome your attachment to things, people, and concepts of the world in order to attain a heightened perspective. Non-attachment doesn't mean being cold as stone; emotions don't cease to exist as you learn to let go. You'll just relate to emotions differently because you'll understand their ephemeral nature.

Those practicing non-attachment no longer pridefully entangle themselves in emotional states by firing up aversion for the 'negative' or craving for the 'positive.' They allow emotions to rise and dissolve, and they don't fuel drama or express distress by engaging in knock-on negative behaviors. Ultimately, they have consummate perspective, which engenders peace of mind. Non-attachment takes considerable practice but virtually everyone has the power to tame their mind through cultivating mindfulness and meditative awareness, which allows you to experience emotions without reacting to them, and to be fearlessly with the world *as it is*. Non-attachment is therefore considered an extremely wise virtue in various Eastern philosophies, such as Jainism, Taoism, and Buddhism. They accept that all physical manifestations of energy and life arise from, and return to, Consciousness, in an eternal, karmic, and cosmic cycle.

My friend Michelle has been in recovery from heroin, crack-cocaine, and alcohol addiction since May 2017. She has an incredible story that can be heard on my Life in Recovery Podcast (Episode 13). This is part of her story in relation to impermanence, which, as far as I can tell, is life's only promise…

I'm a recovering addict, so when speaking or writing on the subject of impermanence, I often share stories relating to my addiction, the behaviors that run alongside it, and how a Twelve Step Program has improved my life dramatically. I have, however, had various experiences not related to my addiction that tie in with the subject of impermanence, such as synchronicities, miracles, 'God-instances,' connection with the universe and a feeling of Oneness. Also, a deeper understanding that the body is finite and dies whereas I am a conscious, aware, eternal life-force that emanates from an infinite universal energy Source. While my body is impermanent, my soul lives on, and has greater potential than I am ever likely to know in this lifetime. I've also had relatable religious experiences, and experiences of practices that have helped me on my journey. I'm continually discovering more, and I feel it is my purpose and quest to stay on this spiritual path and to keep experiencing the peace, connection, and inner wisdom that comes with it.

I first met Ren through my profession. He was a Team Leader for a substance misuse service that I worked very closely with when I was employed as a Peer Mentor (with lived experience) for a partner agency. We conversed at work from time to time but I had no idea Ren was also a recovering addict. After several months of team meeting, and being none the wiser about the similarities we shared, I was at a hard house rave one night with two of my recovery buddies, surrounded by a sea of clubbers – high on drugs and dancing to the beat – when I spotted a familiar face, Ren. He came over and we chatted. It seemed the four of us were the only sober people in the room. As the night progressed, we talked some more, which led to a series of coincidences (God-instances as I've come to know them) that led to Ren asking me to write a segment for this book.

Like me, Ren went down the Twelve Step recovery route, as well as exploring various spiritual practices. Ren told me about the books he'd written and his Life in Recovery Podcast whereby he interviews people in recovery. I read his books in a few days before guesting on his podcast a few weeks later. Ren told me, that night in the rave, that he had been a DJ through his late teens to late twenties, and he introduced me to one of the DJ's at the Rave, Amber D, who he had known for over ten years. She had also written a segment in Ren's book Anonymous God, and it was clear they had a connection, as she greeted him so warmly. The next day, he sent me some of the tracks he had produced, and it turned out we used to do the same circuits back in the day. Whilst he was a DJ, I was on the other side of the DJ box – giving it large! It was highly likely our paths had crossed before. I also found out that Ren's partner Adele hails from the same home-town as me, is the same age, and we went to the same primary school.

The whole experience of getting to know Ren through his books and the podcast interview felt a little surreal, as I identified with so much of his emotions and experiences. It felt as though we had stumbled across each other for a Higher Purpose: to share this message of recovery and impermanence – as I see it now. He had written about the possibility and impact of implementing a Twelve Step Program in schools, and how it could change the course of humanity. I had previously worked on a small project, which had done something very similar and was a huge success. I therefore found Ren's ideas about spiritual education really interesting, as I have explored some of these concepts in my own way and reached the same conclusion. LOVE and CONNECTION; that is where it is at for me, where I feel whole, where I am able to live out my purpose from a well-intentioned place, and be the best version of myself most of the time – living in the solution. It doesn't mean I don't lose my way sometimes, or finding myself *down cul-de-sacs from time to time, off the beaten track, but being connected to a Power greater than myself I am able to find my way back fairly quickly and mostly unscathed.*

One of my earliest memories of realizing there was more to life than we know, was as a young girl when I had ridden my bike over to my nan's house. I fearlessly bounced over curbs as if they weren't there – almost causing an accident when my front tire slipped and I nearly got thrown off in front of an oncoming car. I thought nothing of it and carried on to my nan's, who was feeling heartbroken after my grandad had passed away, and she had decided to call in a spiritualist. After dinner, a lady arrived to do a reading for my nan, and whilst I sat listening, the lady turned to me and said, "Your grandad says you've got to stop racing round on your bike like a maniac and stop bouncing over those curbs or you'll kill yourself!" I was blown away and couldn't believe my ears. There is no way she could have known, as I hadn't mentioned it to my nan. That's when I realized our Soul lives on.

Years later when I was 17, I was travelling alone in Australia, out in the middle of nowhere, staying in a caravan and working on a farm. I'd met a Muslim guy and we'd been out on a date. He and his family were working on the farm and they invited me for dinner at his sister's house. He asked me to wear the Muslim outfit that women wear but I politely declined, saying he met me in a pair of shorts and if that's not acceptable then maybe I am not the girl for him. He said it was no problem but I went to the house for dinner and over the space of a few hours there were several incidents that left me in a state of panic – thinking I was in danger – and that I really needed to get out of there. I left the house and went for a walk to clear my head. I felt very anxious and asked, "What am I going to do? Help me." I had no phone, very little money, and the nearest town was a six-hour-drive, and no one that knew me knew where I was. I was walking by a lake and I suddenly felt my grandad's presence. I felt at peace and that everything would be okay, and I would know what to do when the time came, so I went straight home.

The next day, I went to work, saw the guy and his family and the sense of panic came over me again, but I heard my grandad's voice, "Tell them you have a headache and you are going home." I did that, went back to the caravan, packed my things, and got on the one-and-only coach that went through that area each day. I got off the coach after a ten-hour-journey and found a quiet little back-packer hostel. To my amazement when I walked in, my neighbor Neil (who was like a brother to me and whom I had lived next door to throughout my childhood) was there right in front of me. Neither of us knew the other was travelling in Australia, least of all in the same hostel in that very moment. What are the chances of that? That was when I knew God-instances were possible and I knew my grandad's soul was looking out for me – like Neil did for a week before I got another job and carried on my travels.

As my life progressed and addiction took hold back in the UK, I found myself using drugs to dangerous levels and causing myself unimaginable pain. Almost daily, I used to travel over thirty minutes to Birmingham from my hometown to buy my 'fix.' One particular day, I'd managed to score some heroin and I was in withdrawals, so I couldn't wait to get the drugs coursing through my veins. I went to the toilets in the nearest McDonalds for a 'hit' and felt myself 'going over' straight away. I'd taken too much. I managed to get myself out of the cubicle and across the road before collapsing on a roundabout. When I came to, I was in hospital and a man who I didn't recognize, was there; his name was Michael. He explained he was a drug worker, had seen me collapse, and therefore recognized the signs and managed to get me to A&E in time. As soon as he told me the story and explained how he wanted to make sure I was ok, he disappeared – never to be seen again. It felt like a gift from above that Michael just happened to be in the right place at the right time, and I certainly felt like an invisible force was watching over me, I felt part of the Oneness.

The first time I experienced the feeling I'd been searching for all my life, the feeling of freedom from my mind and connection to all that is, was when I was 18. I was still travelling in Australia and I had decided to go off with a tent on my own and live off the land for a few days, to enjoy the landscape and what nature had to offer. I had been out walking daily and sleeping under the stars at night, and I had no contact with the outside world. After a couple of days, I felt totally connected, internally and externally, to every movement, noise, wave, and particle of energy; the entire universe. It was as if I was completely part of the Whole, moving with it as One. I felt at peace, like I wanted for nothing. I don't remember how long that feeling lasted but I felt totally aware, conscious, present in every moment, and filled with love and connection to all that is. I realized then that I was more than my body and greater than I could ever imagine. I have continued to experience that feeling, sometimes fleetingly when I meditate, sometimes when I follow a Twelve Step Program, and sometimes when I stay connected to nature.

During my recovery, I've been exposed to several teachings that have had a profound impact on my consciousness and my journey including Scientology, Christianity, and Buddhism. I believe there is merit to be found in each teaching, although I personally struggle when I have to put my soul-experience in a box and label it. So, for me, although I can absolutely see the value of each practice, I don't follow one set way, and I aim to stay open-minded, which has served me well. I've been able to draw the good from each philosophy and add them to my spiritual toolbox for daily living.

I first encountered Scientology through a rehab where I went in my first attempt to get 'clean.' I learned many life skills whilst there, practical ways of being and communicating, but one of the most important things I learned was they believe you are a soul with a body. They believe the mind is like a computer with conscious and unconscious parts; analytical and reactive elements that are affected by emotional and physical pain, which causes irrational ways of thinking and behaving that can be counselled-out to gain more freedom from the obsessive state of mind we all seem to suffer from. This then enables you to be at your best and able to handle life and live from cause rather than effect. Scientologists do an exercise very similar to meditation, which I practiced for hundreds of hours over the five years I was there. The purpose of this practice was to rehabilitate the soul and become fully aware and in control of the mind and body, which in turn brings about not only peace but wellness of the body and mind, better control and reaction times, self-awareness, and a higher IQ. I did experience all of those improvements, as I became more extroverted, more analytical in thinking, and able to respond more rationally rather than reacting emotionally to triggers. I definitely got a lot out of this practice and when I explored it further, it goes a lot deeper with spiritual counselling. This practice opened me up to realms of potential I would never have dreamed of, and if I hadn't already cemented the fact of being an infinite soul having a human experience, I certainly would have had that belief as a result of Scientology's teachings.

After leaving Scientology following a relapse on drugs and finding Twelve Step fellowships, I continued on my spiritual journey and explored Buddhism and meditation, which I find extremely beneficial. What I like about Buddhism is that there is no ultimate right or wrong, as morality is something we create for ourselves. I therefore feel able to practice what suits me, and I don't feel like I'm being told what to do like in other spiritual practices. When I meditate I sometimes have that feeling of Oneness that I experienced all those years ago in Australia. My most powerful meditations have come following the reading out of 'step work' through my Twelve Step Program; getting to the truth of who I am and letting go of the rest. Taking time to meditate, and be grateful, has created many-a-powerful experience in the past couple of years. It never ceases to amaze me how connected to miracles, love, and synchronicity I can get when practicing honesty, kindness, and courage on a daily basis.

There is one more experience I would like to share, which if I'm honest, confused me. This experience was through Christianity. I have never been interested in going to church after going to Sunday School as a child, which for me didn't make any sense, and I found it boring. About a year ago (in 2018), I was dating a guy, who I thought was my perfect match. He was in recovery from addiction, he was a hairdresser like me, he worked in a rehab like me, he had a sense of humor, and he was good looking to top it off. He was also a Christian and invited me to a Christian conference in London, which I wouldn't have gone to if it hadn't been for him. On the day we arrived it was disaster after disaster and we didn't make it to the conference. We had to pop out at lunch to go to the bank and get our money sorted, as it had been stolen the day before. My boyfriend and I also decided to break up (but remain friends), as we weren't getting along. On the second day, I sat there thinking, "What on Earth am I doing here? This is not for me." I wasn't enjoying it at all.

We got back on the train to go to the conference and the train broke down. This was one thing too many for me to cope with and I broke down in tears, uncontrollably. I felt totally fed up. A lady came over and said she was a staff member from the conference and asked if she could pray for me. I said yes, then whilst praying she asked if I would like baptizing. Again, I said yes. I had tried so many other things already, why not baptism? She said they were only baptizing at the conference once over the three days, and it happened to be that day at 4pm. I checked the time and it was coming up for 4pm. Suddenly, the train started moving again... it was bizarre.

We arrived at the conference and the lady took me to where they were baptizing, but apparently it was only for the conference staff, so they wouldn't let me in. The lady managed to get me a special pass and I ended up being one of two people to be baptized from a crowd of 10,000 people. It was very moving. My sad, uncontrollable tears turned to healing tears and I went back into the conference feeling connected to every beat of the music and every word spoken. I felt a deep internal healing around my now ex-boyfriend (and my history with men in general), and I came away feeling restored in some peaceful, contented way.

For the next year I went to church regularly. I loved the music and singing but I seemed to shut down when the supposed 'word of God' was being spoken, and I couldn't seem to get into it at all. I decided to go and have some healing at my local church, the purpose of which is to remove the lies you've been told or tell yourself about God, and to replace those lies with truths and gifts from God. I was unsure about it but I went anyway. I uncovered some unhealthy behavior patterns and beliefs that stemmed from childhood, and during the healing session God spoke through me whilst the woman taking the session asked questions and took note of what lies I needed to surrender, and what gifts God would replace the lies with (she didn't use a Bible and she didn't prompt me in any way aside from asking questions). God told me that I am loved more than I know, I am worthy, I am held, I am powerful, and I am a child of the light, who has a strong connection to God. I live in truth and I am a spiritual warrior-daughter that has been given the gift of a Crown of Glory (I had a vision of it being placed on my head), and a Sword of the Spirit, and I have been given a pure heart capable of loving and of being loved. I have also been given the gift of a helping hand.

This experience happened a few weeks ago (October 2019) and it was incredibly powerful. It left me feeling, again, that I am more than my body and that I have a Higher Purpose, which aligns with my soul. Since then, I've definitely had a stronger connection with people in general. Normally, I meet my friends and bare my soul then I feel too vulnerable and I back off and disconnect from them, as I feel that I am different and I don't fit in, and I don't feel worthy of their friendship. I've always struggled maintaining friendships as a result but since that experience, I am less fearful of being myself in front of others and I am able to stand in my truth and not feel judged, which was all lies and self-condemnation anyway. Since the healing, I've also had some honest and open chats with my dad that have mended years of damage; conversations I thought we would never have, and I've moved to a different town and connected with some new people that I would now class as real friends. I am building relationships that I feel have meaning and bring joy to my life, which has helped me open up and be ok with being me, and more accepting of myself and others.

I feel incredibly blessed to have been gifted so many spiritual experiences and I wholeheartedly believe that my impermeant body is superseded by my eternal soul. By being open-minded, I continue to grow and stay connected, acknowledging all of the manifestations of spirit and allowing them in to my human life to keep me in the flow of love, connection, synchronicities, and miracles. This inspires me to be the best version of myself, so I can help myself and others no matter the situation, which brings me peace of mind, as I find solace by trusting in the universe that I'm exactly where I'm meant to be in any given moment. I also trust that everything that has happened (including everyone that crossed my path) was meant to be that way.

As a result of living my life this way, I feel I am a better person; I am more loving, caring, kind, honest, open, willing, humble, assertive, consistent, responsible, and I have courage and faith to undertake the ups-and-downs of daily life. I have been able to rebuild my family relationships and work with other addicts both professionally and in Twelve Step fellowships. I was gifted a way out of addiction and now I have a real purpose in life to give to others what was freely given to me. I let go and let God and I don't try to control outcomes as much as I used to; what will be will be – regardless of how much I try to change it. I have become resilient, grateful, and accepting of myself and others. I can't imagine sleep-walking through life any longer and I wouldn't want my life to be any other way. I am open to learning more, but whether I do or not is okay, as I know that I have everything I could possibly need right now through my connection to Source.

Michelle D

"THROUGH PRIDE WE ARE EVER DECEIVING OURSELVES. BUT DEEP DOWN BELOW THE SURFACE OF THE AVERAGE CONSCIENCE A STILL, SMALL VOICE SAYS TO US, SOMETHING IS OUT OF TUNE"

– Carl Jung (Swiss psychiatrist and psychoanalyst)

LESSON THREE: PRIDE

On 'day 3' of the retreat I had to ask for help. I was suffering terribly with a head-cold, so I had to ask one of the helpers to get me some decongestion medication, as I didn't think I could last seven more days without it. This was the catalyst for a huge insight on pride. I was reminded that most people don't like asking for help because they don't want to appear weak or needy, and that was my problem for so many years. I was definitely full of pride before my emotional breakdown in 2010, which led to me starting my journey of recovery and repeatedly asking for help in a variety of Twelve Step fellowships.

Not asking for help is an example of false-pride. Self-seeking and self-centering in its essence, false (or hubristic) pride causes more interpersonal conflicts for the human race than any other emotion. False pride is the exacerbation of self-importance and consists of feeling superior to others while being infatuated with the few qualities we possess, and fantasizing that we possess those we lack. For example: I might judge someone for being overweight while simultaneously being infatuated with the way I look and fantasizing that I have the body of Adonis when I clearly don't! False pride can hinder personal progress if we think we have all the answers because in order for us to learn, we must first admit that we don't know everything. From Proverbs 16:18 of the *King James Bible*, "Pride goeth before destruction, and a haughty spirit before a fall," meaning that people who are self-aggrandizing, overconfident, or arrogant, will at some stage, metaphorically 'fall down' and experience much suffering. This happened to me in 2009 when I hit an emotional rock-bottom after I stopped drinking alcohol and initially refused to get the help I needed.

There's nothing wrong with authentic pride; being proud of yourself, your appearance, and your accomplishments, but humbling yourself regularly will ensure that you don't succumb to false pride. Asking for help is the first step down the path toward false pride's opposite, humility; having a modest view of your own importance. By gaining humility, you'll realize that you're not the center of the universe and the entire world *doesn't* revolve around you, and that you are a small but integral part of the universal web of interdependence that we call humanity. Buddhist master, poet, and teacher, Dilgo Khyentse Rinpoche said, "If you keep your mind humble, pride will vanish like morning mist."

Humility is not about thinking less of yourself, it's about thinking of yourself less. I feel the importance of humility in contemporary society is seldom considered and neither is the significance of honesty, open-mindedness, and willingness (H.O.W), or personal powerlessness over people, places, and things (Step One of The Twelve Step Program). These concepts can be overwhelmingly profound when applied in our everyday lives. H.O.W and powerlessness are inextricably linked to humility. We can naturally assume that we're all-powerful until we make a truly honest, open-minded, and comprehensive assessment of ourselves and realize our limitations. If you really think about it, we only ever truly have power over our own beliefs, attitudes, perspectives, actions, and reactions. We can control nothing else, yet we attempt to control most things because hardly anything is the way we actually want it to be. People, places, and things (such as rush-hour traffic or the weather) rarely dance to our tune, which is why acceptance is the key to equanimity; accept the things you cannot change.

We are seemingly free to make decisions but we definitely have no control over outcomes. Personal powerlessness over people, places, and things is merely an accurate observation of how it really is to live in the world, and shouldn't be confused with helplessness, which suggests weakness, over-dependency on other people, or an inability to help oneself. Acceptance of personal powerlessness is essential in overcoming false pride, which is a cumbersome obstacle on the path to peace of mind – and continuously raises its ugly head on my journey. These days, however, I ask people for help all the time, and I honestly own up if I don't know the answer to something – rather than being a 'know-it-all' – and I remain open-minded, teachable, and ever-willing to learn.

Often, the obsession with our self-image, which we feel we *have* to project, is so strong that we stop questioning the validity of appearances and we endlessly seek better ways to appear (especially on social media, such as Facebook, Twitter, and Instagram). The word humility evolved from the Latin 'humus,' which means to be grounded. Humility is not a lesser form of humiliation but the key to accepting your relative insignificance in an infinite universe. It is a nourishing ingredient that brings a state of serenity, which is essential to lasting happiness. If you are humble and modest then you are less likely to be proud and arrogant, and more likely to be considerate and respectful of others. Despite occasionally succumbing to false-pride, this is how I try to live my life – one day at a time.

If you are a humble member of the human race, educated in the principles of love and service (the action of helping or doing work for others with no reward), your main ambition in life is more likely to simply 'be of service' to your fellows, helping them however you can. As a person amongst people in community, rather than a proud individual in a detached society, you might ask, "What's best for myself, those closest to me, and the wider community?" rather than, "What's in it for me." True love is wanting maximum spiritual growth for another person, despite what that might entail for you.

I think many people believe that material pleasures and satisfactions bring lasting happiness, but this is a myth. If comfort was the way to contentment then all those who live in a mansion and own a luxurious car would always be peaceful and happy. Conversely, someone who lives in a small rented apartment and travels to work every day second-class on a train, should rarely experience peace of mind or contentment, but we know this isn't the case. Peace of mind and contentment are dependent on your mental state, which has less to do with external factors and more to do with your response to your emotional state. One of my most peaceful experiences to date was sat on a bus one summer morning in 2015 on my way to central London for work. I'd been practicing meditation for about six months and when I awoke that morning my perception of the world had altered from analogue to Super-HD, I felt absolutely serene, and unconditional love for everyone I encountered. A spiritual experience (explained in detail in my book *Anonymous God*), which lasted for four days.

Spiritual practices, such as meditation, mindfulness, prayer, and yoga are a prerequisite if you want to avoid or overcome mental illness and enjoy peace of mind and lasting happiness because they foster both self-love and altruism. One need only think of other people before yourself to lead a more productive, purposeful, meaningful, happy, and fulfilling life. It's quite as simple as that, but for a naturally selfish person like me, it's not always so easy to think of others before myself.

We are *all* obligated to help each other, as we can't 'do life' on our own. Acknowledging that you can't live without the help of others is the first phase in humbly admitting that you are powerless over people, places, and things. As I've already postulated, you have no control over other people, as we are all seemingly free to do as we wish. You have no control over places, such as the functioning of the city in which you live, and you have no control over things, such as traffic-jams or the weather. Crucially, as I learned on the Vipassana retreat, you also have no control over the thoughts and emotions that arise within you like waves on a limitless ocean. However, you can learn to respond to emotions and thoughts in a healthy manner rather than reacting to them without consideration, which is the root of most interpersonal conflict. Responding patiently rather than reacting impulsively to your own thoughts and emotions is how you develop equanimity and ultimately emotional intelligence.

This is what I've been working on since 2017 in my relationship with Adele. It has taken external help in the form of traditional medicines and relationship counselling but we are both much better at responding rather than reacting as a result of the work we have done so far.

When you attempt to influence, direct, or manipulate people, you're forcing your will upon them, and this usually ends in frustration, as we simply don't know what is best for another human. If you try to exert force over anything, you are presuming that person, place, or thing is not already in alignment with a Higher Power/Higher Purpose. You are in fact 'playing God' by attempting to control things rather than letting go and allowing life to flow. Fear, control, manipulation, and power are the opposites of love, faith, compassion, and humility. Each cannot exist without its interconnected counterpart.

The Grand Design of life cannot be observed from within; the whole painting cannot be observed from inside the paint. We can only trust that the Architect of the Grand Design, The Painter, has things under control, and all looks well from His/Her/Its perspective. Everything is as it should be at all times, all is well, and acceptance is therefore the answer to all our problems – no matter how big or overwhelming they may seem. As recovering alcoholic Dr. Paul O wrote in the 'Big Book' *Alcoholics Anonymous*, "When we are disturbed, it is because we find some person, place, thing or situation – some fact of life – unacceptable to us, and we can find no serenity until we accept that person, place, thing or situation as being exactly the way it is at that moment. We need to concentrate not so much on what needs to be changed in the world as on what needs to be changed in ourselves and our own attitudes."

Acceptance empowers you, as it signals to the universe that you have surrendered to the 'plan,' and you are ready to move on to the next life lesson. In my experience, the universe is both alive and conscious and seems to work with people to help them fulfill their life's mission by presenting the perfect obstacles, difficulties, and opportunities that their Consciousness needs in order to evolve, ascend, and transcend their human limitations. Resistance will not move you forward, nor will it eliminate the undesirable. There's no need for you to waste your energy trying to change people, places, or things, and there's no point in placing great emphasis on expectations, as expectations most often lead to disappointment because they are the opposite of acceptance. There's no point in trying to change your partner, child, family member, colleague, or friend; they all have their own life lessons to learn. Accept the fact that most people do not change until not changing is more painful. You only have the power to change yourself. Self-transformation, change, is pivotal to emotional/spiritual growth and contentment. Change is *inevitable* and the only true constant in life. If you can find composure amidst the change, you will be contented.

How we change and grow, not *why* we should change, is the fundamental question that concerns us when we are working on ourselves. Change and grow simply for the good of yourself and those around you rather than for any material gain. The way that we change is a process of awareness through observation and understanding (a minimum of 30 minutes introspection/meditation/mindfulness per day, plus inventory/journaling), acceptance through approval and forgiveness (a positive mental attitude toward ourselves and others), and change through action (love and service). The 3 A's: awareness, acceptance, action. This is one of my life mantra's.

One of the first fruits of meditation is emotional balance, which, when practiced continually and diligently, is a state that helps one develop emotional intelligence. I can honestly say, thanks to practicing meditation, I am much more equanimous now than I used to be. Adele and I still have arguments but I'm rarely quick to anger, and I can calmly defuse most situations and deal with them intuitively. Prior to recovery this was an impossibility because I was full of pride and anger, and I was only using the rational part of my mind that gets me in the most trouble! This all changed when I developed a relationship with my Higher Power through the science of love; prayer and meditation, and my rational mind took a back seat to intuition (God-consciousness). Ironically, I think I stopped believing in God when I reached the age of reason (around eleven years of age), which coincided with my emotional unbalancing that became more and more noticeable with an ever-increasing anxiety, as my gradual disconnection from Consciousness began.

To experience peace of mind and contentment, it's essential that you develop emotional balance. If you don't, it's very likely you'll use substances such as nicotine, alcohol, cannabis, cocaine, amphetamine or heroin (or behaviors such as gambling, compulsive over-exercising, compulsive over-working, compulsive shopping, compulsive sex, or compulsive over-eating), to help you cope with your emotional disorder that every human being experiences in varying degrees. There is a danger that you might develop a "curious mental twist" (as mentioned in the Big Book *Alcoholics Anonymous*), which is the penultimate stage of addiction, whereby you become psychologically dependent on behaviors and/or highly addictive, poisonous substances that grant you temporary relief from your perceived problems. Having faith in a Higher Power that helps you overcome problems rather than using substances and/or behaviors to avoid problems, is a healthy way to grow emotionally and develop emotional balance rather than attempting to attain equanimity through behaviors and/or substances.

To develop emotional balance, first, it's necessary to understand what emotional (inward) disorder feels like, as outward disorder is obvious to spot and looks like: an untidy living space, not washing and grooming regularly, often being late for appointments, regularly arguing with people, and not brushing one's teeth every day. Inward disorder is not so easy to spot, as we all experience, react, and respond differently to the vast range of human emotions. Some people are less emotionally balanced than others and some people have a lower level of emotional intelligence. All people are emotionally unavailable a lot of the time – when they are 'lost' in their SMART phone or TV for example. No matter how emotionally intelligent you are, however, you *will* experience emotional disorder at some point in your life due to bereavement (a period of mourning after a loss – especially after the death of a loved one), abandonment (feeling abandoned by family or friends), relationship breakdowns (such as divorce or splitting up with a partner), a period of sickness/illness affecting the body or mind, or high-anxiety provoking situations (which are subjective), such as exams, interviews, public speaking, or a first date. Most of this happens on the emotional and mental level and can therefore remain hidden from plain sight. For example, no one knew how much I was struggling with my mental health before I hit my emotional rock-bottom in 2010. Had it not been for Twelve Step fellowships, I definitely would have drunk alcohol again and possibly might have committed suicide if the emotional and psychic pain became too much to bear, as it does for some unfortunate people.

According to Samaritans, there were 6,507 suicides in the UK in 2018, which was a 10.9% increase from the previous year. Men are three times as likely to die by suicide than women, and men aged 45-49 have the highest rate of suicides. The rate of deaths among under 25's also increased by 23.7%, reaching 730 deaths in 2018.

Accepting life on life's terms in the face of bereavement, abandonment, relationship breakdowns, illness, and anxiety, can be mastered by turning your problems over to the care of a Higher Power (of your own understanding) through prayer and meditation. Difficult emotions, such as sorrow, uncertainty, anger, and fear – as a response to the things in life that you would rather not happen to you – will no longer overwhelm or debilitate you if you learn to 'turn them over' to your Higher Power, as you will be gifted the strength to face these difficulties and overcome them. This has been my experience.

When harmful habits such as smoking, drinking alcohol, or using other drugs get 'out of control,' they can cause increasing amounts of stress, which adds to the general stresses of daily life. American addiction expert Dr. Kevin McCauley suggests that all addictions can be explained as a response to the deployment in the brain of the 'stress hormones' cortisol, adrenaline, and norepinephrine that people generally described as feeling, "stressed out," or simply, "stressed." Inward disorder (stress) can lead to behavioral and substance misuse as a coping mechanism, plus interpersonal conflicts and health problems that create even more stress. Inward disorder can therefore prevent you from reaching your true potential and deter you from your Higher Purpose. If you become aware of an aspect of your life that is creating problems or stress, you must acknowledge this *before* you can determine how to take steps to overcome it. If you could overcome a problem on your own, you already would have done so, and therefore you wouldn't need any help – and you probably wouldn't have reached this point in this book.

If you concede to your innermost-self that you *do* need help with certain aspects of life, you can enjoy the immediate feeling of relief that comes with the act of surrender; relinquishing the desire for control. Giving up control can be an emotionally painful struggle. Acceptance comes with the knowledge that you will receive the strength from your Higher Power to survive life's problems, and that your emotional wounds *will* be healed. You can then face your problems head on, and this, in turn, brings emotional stability, as you realize you *can* cope with life's difficulties.

Stability will come when you learn to give your help freely, not from demanding what you think you should receive from other people and your Higher Power. At the root of every emotional disturbance you have is a selfish demand. In other words, you believe you need some person, place, or thing, to make you happy, when in fact you do not. If you give up demanding, and stop resisting the flow of life itself by turning your compulsions, and your demands, over to your Higher Power, this will bring you peace of mind.

Admitting that you are powerless over people, places, and things, and that you can be outwardly and inwardly unmanageable, requires that you observe this powerlessness and unmanageability in your life *before* you can admit it. By witnessing and understanding your own powerlessness and unmanageability you become more self-aware and able to overcome life's inevitable problems rather than avoiding them, or worse, numbing them with substances and/or compulsive behaviors. People who become physically dependent on substances do so because they can't cope with life. They avoid their problems and attempt to nullify their pain and unwittingly become addicted to their 'crutch,' which they falsely perceive is supporting them.

We often know that life could be better and more enjoyable but we are accustomed to the way things are, and we don't feel like we have the power to change them. You might be powerless over feelings of resentment, insecurity, anxiety, or depression. You might also be powerless over smoking, using alcohol and other drugs, social media, gambling, or sex. You are not, however, powerless over making a decision to change. Pain and suffering from personal problems is usually the trigger for change but we don't have to wait until life becomes insufferable to take the first steps toward a better life. If a child asks for help and they do not get the help they need (which in my experience working in the health sector is a much more common occurrence than one might think), or the help simply doesn't come, this can be extremely traumatizing for them. It's no wonder, therefore, that so many adults, who were once children that did not get their basic needs met, don't dare to ask for help for fear of rejection. If you were one of those children, please do not delay in asking for help with your suffering and, in time, you might help others.

"NEVER BE AFRAID TO TRUST AN UNKNOWN FUTURE TO A KNOWN GOD"

- Corrie ten Boom (Dutch watchmaker and writer)

LESSON FOUR: TURNING IT OVER

When I first came to believe in a Higher Power, I suppose I was lucky that I was agnostic, and mine wasn't a deep-seated block against God that I often see in people who are atheist. in my experience, some people's will to disbelieve in a Higher Power can be so powerful that they prefer to suffer rather than conduct an open-minded and experimental spiritual quest for God. Beaten into complete defeat by anxiety, depression, and drugs, I found myself surrounded by happy people in Twelve Step fellowships who spoke truth from their hearts and accepted me without judgement. Feeling safe, I was then able to surrender – initially to the group of recovering alcoholics (which is like a 'hive mind') – and then to The Twelve Step Program and a Higher Power (of my own understanding). The group is no longer my Higher Power because the group cannot always be there in times of need like my Higher Power can. As I slowly came to believe, I subsequently found myself in a new dimension – a brighter world of faith and spirit – as the greyness of depression slowly subsided and I became God-conscious.

Coming to believe in a Higher Power is a personal journey; an open mind is essential. If you have trouble believing in the concept of 'God,' your group (i.e. your meeting or spiritual assembly) is undoubtedly a Power greater than yourself, and together, providing you're all pulling in the same direction, you can collectively overcome life's problems. This is how Twelve Step fellowships, such as Alcoholics Anonymous, Narcotics Anonymous, Overeaters Anonymous, Gamblers Anonymous, Sex Addicts Anonymous, Alanon (for the family of alcoholics and addicts), and Alateen (for younger relatives and friends of alcoholics and addicts) work for people (including atheists) to help their members recover. They stick together and help each other whenever and however they can, as the group is more powerful than the individual alone. Connection is key, and for those already affiliated with a religion, Twelve Step fellowships only serve to deepen that connection from my observations.

Once you have faith in a Higher Power, it's less likely you'll feel alone or disconnected from the rest of humanity – like I did for many years. The reason we (in Twelve Step fellowships) come to believe in a Higher Power, and work together as part of a group, is because 'doing life' on our own – without help – can lead to anxiety, depression, disconnection, isolation, and loneliness, and ultimately addiction and death. The lonely and disconnected individual is far more likely to abuse harmful substances and practice addictive behaviors in an attempt to block out depressive feelings of loneliness and sadness at having little sincere human connection, which I believe we all crave in varying degrees. We all need some form of community to feel 'part of' and people tend to thrive when they feel part of a 'tribe.'

I believe that most mental illness is caused by the feeling of separateness, with fear at its core, and most physical illnesses are the body's response to mental sickness. If more people adopted a spiritual program, mental health issues, substance and behavioral addictions, suicide rates, and crime, would begin to decrease. Mental health issues and addiction cannot thrive if the population is connected to each other with love, and fear cannot flourish in a loving environment. Fear and love are opposites, and the two base emotions from which all other emotions stem. Bearing in mind that all emotions are energy vibrating at different frequencies, all positively charged emotions such as joy, gratitude, and serenity stem from love, and all negatively charged emotions such as resentment, anger, and jealousy stem from fear. Prior to physical dependence, addicts attempt to medicate their mental illness with addictive substances and/or behaviors, which can be very harmful to the body and mind.

Addiction is primarily a progressive emotional and mental disorder, whereby an addict uses a substance and/or behavior to medicate themselves, which can lead to self-harm and suicide if the symptoms are not treated.

Patient X, for example, who attempted suicide in June 2018, as a result of overdosing on pharmaceutical medications obtained on the 'black market,' was hoping that he wouldn't wake up. Patient X was unable to quantify the amounts, but he reported that he used crack-cocaine and heroin two-to-three times a week in an attempt to manage the voices he heard as a result of his schizophrenia. Patient X advised that he heard three command voices; a young child, his dad, and the priest who sexually abused him when he was 8 years of age. Two weeks before he overdosed on heroin and died in December 2018, Patient X stated to his drug worker that he continually re-lived the sexual trauma over and over in his mind and he had never spoken to anyone in any real detail about the abuse.

Emotional disorder will always progress to mental illness if it's not treated with some form of counselling or therapy in my opinion. If we continue to experience this inward unmanageability, eventually our mind will seek out the temporary sense of ease and comfort it will receive from performing certain behaviors or from using substances. Anyone can become addicted to substances and/or behaviors at any time, as no one is immune from addiction. One only has to consider the devastating effects of drugs and alcohol on the indigenous populations around the globe. Once introduced, these substances have decimated entire cultures. There is never any guarantee that once a person starts using a drug they will ever be able to stop, however, if you're emotionally balanced and you have honest, unconditional, loving connections with other people, it's less likely that you'll abuse substances. You'll have the ability to deal with your emotions by talking about them rather than needing to escape them through the bottle, pipe, spliff, or syringe.

Finding a Power greater than yourself that will help you overcome life's problems is, therefore, of paramount importance. But where and how are you to find such a Power? Religions talk of God (or Gods) and atheism rejects the belief in any deities. Why not choose your own conception of God? Build a unique and personal relationship with your Higher Power, which can be anything you want Him/Her/It to be – providing you can communicate with Him/Her/It through prayer and meditation, as this is the process of 'turning it over.' You can also learn to rely upon help and support from members of your spiritual group, which you will gain as a result of sharing your problems and not bottling up unmanageable emotions. People in Twelve Step fellowships often say their Higher Power speaks to them through people, which is why 'God' is not a necessity, but a Higher Power is.

Having the humility to admit that you need help to get through life, that everyone needs help, and that some people need more help than others is an enlightened perspective. Conversely, you can be of service to people just by listening to them without judgment, and accepting them for who they are in their uniqueness and in their differences from you. This is how we cultivate compassion and how we grow toward loving all humans as our brothers and sisters in a global community – regardless of race, creed, or ethnicity. The process of listening and getting to know each other can be very interesting and enjoyable, and can distract us from our perceived problems, as we begin to understand that everyone has problems and all our problems can be overcome with combined help from each-other and with faith in a Higher Power.

'Let go and let God' (as you understand Him/Her/It), or 'turn it over,' simply means that you allow your life to play out *as it is*. Don't attempt to control the outcomes and have faith that your Higher Power will look after you. An effective practice to help you evolve toward this way of living is to drop the word 'should' from your vocabulary. "He *should* have done this," and, "It *should* have been like that," isn't conducive to a happy and peaceful life, as you're assuming things are not exactly as they're meant to be in any given circumstance. Every problem we come across in life is an opportunity to learn something and grow emotionally. Most often we can't see the 'bigger picture' until many months, or even years later. Emotional disorder dissipates the more we learn to let go of fear, which manifests itself as worry, anxiety, and self-doubt. If you're scared, ask your Higher Power for help in learning how to face and let go of your fears and speak to your fellows openly and honestly. Dare to be vulnerable. It works if you work it.

As an example, my step-daughter Lily was about to swim 100 meters to gain a certificate in 2017. Prior to the examination, Lily was anxious, and just before she entered the pool, she felt scared that she wouldn't be able to swim 100 metres continuously without stopping. Her mom said to her, "Don't worry Lily, it's ok if you fail but you'll be fine. Just do your best." Lily heard her mom and said to herself, "I *will* be fine. Please (Higher Power), help me to complete my 100 meter swim." Lily prayed to her Higher Power by encouraging her innermost self (Consciousness). She completed her swim and was awarded her 100-metre certificate. Afterwards, she wondered why she was ever worried in the first place. That little seed of self-doubt rapidly turned into worry, then anxiety, then upset, but all Lily needed to do was ask for help, let go of the outcome, and try her best, which she did. Had she not completed her 100-meter swim, it wouldn't have been the end of the world. She could have simply kept trying until she accomplished her goal – just like her younger sister Issy did to achieve her 50-meter certificate on the same day.

Having an internal conversation with your inner-most self is no different to praying. When you pray, your ego is essentially surrendering to Consciousness (intuition/God's will). If you can align your will with God's will then I think things are more likely to go well for you in life. The solution to your pain, therefore, is developing faith in a Higher Power (of your own understanding), so you can 'turn over' the problems you would normally try to resolve with your own mind and your own will power. This might not make any sense to you because you think the answer to your problems is to blow off some steam or zone-out by going out and getting drunk and/or 'high,' or gambling, or shopping, or having sex, or eating junk food, or switching off in front of the TV, but it really isn't. It's the same with all temporary distractions from reality; the underlying problems never get resolved. Instead, I suggest turning your problems over to the care of your Higher Power and allowing Him/Her/It to solve them for you. To attain a true and lasting feeling of freedom and serenity that doesn't go hand-in-hand with an emotional or physical hang-over, let go of control and open your mind to something that is far greater than yourself, which will humble you.

Prayer, meditation, and mindfulness are my vehicles to peace of mind. I acknowledge my Higher Power mindfully throughout each day, and I pray and meditate formally every morning and every night. For 'turning it over' to work, it's crucial that you learn to let go *absolutely*. Before you begin your meditation, start with a simple enquiry by asking yourself, "What is here now when there are no problems to solve?..." This will calm your mind and allow you to be consciously aware, so you can observe your breath. Relax and breathe deeply, in-and-out, through your nose (ideally). Concentrate on your breath, and when you lose concentration, come back to your breath.

Following meditation, this is a suggested prayer to help you turn over your will and your life to the care of your Higher Power:

Higher Power, I offer myself to you,
to build with me and to do with me as you will,
relieve me from the bondage of self,
so I might better do your will,
take away my difficulties,
that victory over them may bear witness to those I will help,
with your power, your strength and your way of life,
let me do your will always.

My friend Mark has been in recovery from alcoholism since September 2007. This is his story in relation to 'turning it over'…

Before we can turn our will and our lives over to the care of something much greater than ourselves, we have to attain a belief that there is a Power, or 'spirit of the universe,' that is guiding us through this and every part of our journey. This is no small task for the alcoholic who thought that they were at the very center of everything and in control of their life, and dare I say it, everyone else's. We can find ourselves in a chicken and egg scenario quite quickly in early recovery, as we struggle with the concepts of developing a faith and trust. How can we trust anyone, let alone find a faith to place our entire existence in the hands of a spiritual being, even when we are reassured by others that all will be well?

I can hear the hecklers from the back of the room already, "That is very well for you but what about my sick child, my failing business, my disability, my failed marriage, my homelessness, my mental health problems and the abuse I suffered as a child." As alcoholics, we have a never-ending list of excuses that keep us distant from our Higher Power. Unfortunately, when we embark upon the journey of recovery, this does not mean that we are immune to life's twists and turns and the suffering that goes hand in hand of living life on life's terms. We are not entering into a contract with God that says now we are exploring sobriety we will get everything we want. We are often given all that we need though, if we remain patient and have faith in our Higher Power. More often than not, being given exactly what we need does not sit comfortably with us!

How do we find the faith to trust something greater than ourselves, especially early on? For me I look back to the first day I came into Alcoholics Anonymous. In reflection I did not start that day out by combing my hair in the mirror and saying to myself,

"This is it, today is the day. It is time for change." No. I started the day as I always did, wondering how I was going to get the most out of other people with as little input into life from myself. As a result of this I found myself in an A.A meeting washed up like bits of flotsam and jetsam amongst all of the plastic on some vast beach. But how did I get here? My 'Step One' (we admitted we were powerless over alcohol – that our lives had become unmanageable) clearly showed me the countless times I should have died as an active alcoholic/addict but something had saved me time and time again. When this was gently pointed out to me by my sponsor, I could not deny the fact that for some reason, unclear to myself, I was being given a final chance of a sober existence and – in no way shape or form – was this down to me in anyway. For me this was the first step into a world of faith not dependent upon anything else and the beginning of trying to understand the Step Three prayer: "God, I offer myself to thee-to build with me and do with me as thou wilt. Relieve me of the bondage of self, that I may better do thy will. Take away my difficulties, that victory over them may bear witness to those I would help of Thy power, Thy Love and Thy way of life. May I do Thy will always."

It is worth mentioning that the word God is used here (as you understand It). You get to choose your very own personal concept of a Higher Power. It does not have to be related to any religious denomination. For myself, being quite a complex character that can over complicate things, over the years I have simplified this prayer, using it each morning asking the God of my understanding, "What would you like me to do? And how would you like me to do it?" I usually know if I am doing God's will, as it is not a struggle, and I don't need to try and force outcomes to suit me. I have tried many things – thinking that they were God's will for me. Most have usually resulted in a great deal of suffering and have meant a complete change in direction and approach to life.

On my journey, I have done a great deal of work on self-compassion and understanding that suffering is directly related to how much I resist pain. I have a long-term chronic health condition that has meant I have endured a life of chronic pain for over four decades. I used to despise this illness as it robbed me of all my hopes and dreams. During my first year of sobriety I was introduced to a man who started to teach me how to use meditation. He helped me learn to sit with my pain, both physical and emotional. Over the years, I have come to accept that I am disabled and to stop fighting against my condition. I no longer work 100 hours per week and my fantasies of standing on a podium with colorful garlands slung around my neck, flanked by bikini clad women, have gently dissolved away with my suffering about a life that could have been.

This acceptance of my life has been a slow process though and has not been reached over night. There has been a grieving process that I had to go through. There has often been no human solution to my suffering. This has meant that in the darkest times the only comfort that existed was the relationship that had grown between me and my Higher Power. I had to learn to trust fully in my Higher Power and His will for me, even when it has not been what I wanted. I had to undergo many spinal procedures, some of which have involved me being awake while they were carried out. On those occasions the medical teams that were supporting me were shocked at the calm persona that they witnessed, all of which was the result of many months of prayer and meditation, insuring I had turned my life over fully to the care of my Higher Power.

The only time I suffer today is when I am trying to push my life in a certain direction that suits me. This is utterly exhausting and always a complete waste of time, as I have to retrace my steps and go in the direction I should have gone originally – but didn't look attractive to me at the time! I am gradually beginning to understand that my disability and my experience is my gift. I am beginning to understand that, through turning my will and my life over, I am given opportunities when I am ready for them. Only now that I have ceased fighting, and taken time to commune with my Higher Power, am I of use to Him to carry out His will.

A short while ago, when I was unable to work, I was struggling with the concept of purpose or identity, as so many of us think we are what we do. I had a conversation with a good friend in A.A, who had outlived his predicted death date from his cancer by well over ten years. He too suffered from pain due to his condition. I expressed to him how hopeless I felt, as the first thing people ask you is, "What do you do." He smiled at me and said gently, "Why don't you say to them, you do what you can." This was a suggestion that was so simple and yet delivered with such compassion and wisdom that I felt my frustration and suffering melt away. It clearly reminded me that I have a primary purpose to 'stay sober and help other alcoholics achieve sobriety.' What greater purpose could there be than to help others that are suffering.

I continue to turn my will and my life over to the God of my understanding on a daily basis to ensure that I am not wasting energy inefficiently, so that I can be of greatest use in any given moment to those around me. I must remember however, that I turn over my entire life, not just aspects of it that suit me. This is my morning prayer... A Knight's Prayer: "My Lord, I am ready on the threshold of this new day, to go forth armed with Thy power, seeking adventure on the highroad, to right wrong, to overcome evil, to suffer wounds and endure pain if need be, but in all things to serve Thee bravely, faithfully, joyfully, that at the end of the day's labor, kneeling for Thy blessing, Thou mayest find no blot upon my shield."

Mark C

"FEEDING THE EGO IS STARVING THE WISDOM, THE CHOICE IS YOURS"

- Efrat Cybulkiewicz (Venezuelan artist)

LESSON FIVE: EGO-DEFLATION

Attempting to control people, places, and things is too strenuous for the mind and makes the mind chaotic; wild thoughts can lead to wild behavior. Anything that dominates our thoughts, anything we obsess over, can drive us crazy, then our lives can become chaotic as we begin to act crazily. Most of our troubles, therefore, are of our own making – and stem from this cognitive unmanageability. When we are 'wrapped up' in our thoughts, we are not present for our lives, and we therefore become emotionally and mentally unavailable to those around us. In the worst cases, we can become selfish and self-seeking, isolated and useless, because we are obsessed with ourselves and getting what we think we need to be happy. Life becomes all about what TV program, app, or YouTube video we're obsessed with? What clothes or shoes we *must* have? Self-centered distractions can prevent real connection on a deeply human level. To avoid this self-obsession, aim for humility and deflate your ego, which leads to peace of mind and contentment as a by-product of thinking more about other people and their needs ahead of your own.

Taking 'moral inventory' is a method of ego-deflation that I learned in Twelve Step fellowships. By discovering and analyzing my 'defects of character' (moral and psychological weaknesses and shortcomings) I came to understand how extremes in my instinctive drives cause me lots of problems. It's very important that once you decide to 'take inventory,' you write it all down in a systematic way, because misguided moral inventory can result in guilt, grandiosity, blaming others, and self-justification, which can be a hindrance to your emotional growth on your quest for contentment. Honesty, and a willingness to take stock of one's more favorable and less favorable attributes, brings self-awareness and an appropriate level of self-esteem that might be the beginning of a valuable daily practice.

We don't want to kill the ego, we just want to deflate it and right-size it, so we can stabilize emotionally. Self-review is essential if you're going to evolve healthily in the emotional and psychological sense. To develop humility, it's necessary that you gain some perspective on how your less desirable qualities – mainly selfish, self-seeking, dishonest, and fearful behaviors – affect you and others. If you decide to take regular inventory, your life will take on deeper meaning and purpose, as your perspective and motives will change. The best way to approach 'taking inventory' is to think of it like a business taking stock. Starting with a list of your fears, then a list of your resentments (toward people, places, and things), followed by a list of people whom you've had relationships with. You'll see, in black and white, those personal characteristics that hold you back from being the best version of yourself and from having more successful inter-personal relationships.

Fear, or aversion (as S.N Goenka consistently termed it on the retreat), is a feeling of anxiety concerning the outcome of something, or the safety of someone (including yourself). Fear is a feeling induced by perceived danger or threat, which causes a change in metabolic and organ functions, and ultimately a change in behavior, such as fleeing, hiding, or freezing from perceived traumatic events. The opposite of fear is love. When looking at your fears, write them all down, then ask yourself: why are you fearful and what would your loving Higher Power (or your Higher Self) have you be instead? As an example: if you're fearful of public speaking because you think people might find you unintelligent, your Higher Power would have you be confident (providing you are well prepared), and believing that you *are* intelligent and that you *can* make a positive attempt at public speaking. You must then practice 'turning it over' by asking your Higher Power for confidence rather than running on self-will, which empties you of power, leaving you needing a 'fix' after the event. This will enable you to accomplish the things you feel you can't accomplish on will power alone without using a substance and/or behavior to compensate for the power you lack. It's a very simple process, which has served me well in interviews, presentations, competitions, and examinations over the years of my recovery.

Resentment, which stems from fear, is bitter indignation at having been treated unfairly, and feels like irritation, discontentment, animosity, hate, envy, jealousy, and ultimately anger and rage. Resentment is inextricably linked to self-righteousness. It arises when we think we are right and the other person is wrong, but resentment only hurts you; analogous to drinking poison and expecting the other person to die. Ask yourself this question: do you want to be right or do you want to be happy? If you want to enjoy real peace of mind, you must progressively overcome resentments.

The trick to overcoming resentment is: once you've written down the name of the person, place, or thing, and the reason why you are resentful in the first place, write down how you were affected. Was it your pride, self-esteem, self-worth, personal relations, sex-relations, or financially? Most importantly, dismiss the other person entirely, then write down what *your* part was in the resentment? Write down how you were selfish, self-seeking, dishonest, and frightened? Where were you to blame? And what could you change for future reference?

Understanding the definition of selfishness, self-seeking behaviors, dishonesty, and fear, cultivates self-awareness, which is vital to the process of change. When looking at selfishness, ask yourself what was your motive behind the behavior and what did you hope to gain – possibly at the expense of another? When looking at self-seeking behavior, ask yourself what you felt you needed or what you hoped to achieve that you thought would make you happy? When looking at dishonesty, ask yourself how were you being deceitful or fraudulent? Have you ever acted in the same way toward that person or someone else? When looking at fear, ask yourself how did you feel threatened physically or emotionally? Was the fear rational or irrational?

Paradoxically, in the majority of your resentments, you'll find that you actually have some part to play. For example: I was resentful toward a woman who had cheated on me with another man. My pride was hurt, my self-esteem was affected, my personal relations suffered and my sex relations were damaged. But once I wrote it down and looked at my part, I could see that I had been selfish because I did not give her the attention she deserved and I was often flirting with other women. I had been self-seeking because I needed her absolute attention to make me feel good about myself. I had been dishonest because I had cheated on other women, so who was I to judge? And I was frightened because I felt like I could no longer trust women, as they would all hurt me. What did I need to change? I needed to accept that I had been cheated on and that it was simply my karma, and have faith for future reference that if I remain faithful to a partner, they will remain faithful to me.

Most of our problems happen in relationships, therefore, we need to look at how *we* can change *our* behavior so that we might have healthier interpersonal relationships in the future. Ultimately the buck stops with *you*. This might be difficult to reconcile initially but the more you practice taking inventory, the more you'll see that you are at the center of the majority of your problems.

For the third part of your moral inventory, write down the names of all the people you have had relationships with, what harms you caused them, and the reasons why? Where had you been selfish, dishonest, or inconsiderate? Did you arouse jealousy, suspicion, or bitterness? Where were you at fault? What should you have done instead? This process will give you a clear picture of where you are going wrong in your relationships and what you need to change to improve them. Again, very simple but *very* effective.

Taking moral inventory can be an emotionally painful experience. You might write down a resentment, whereby you had no part to play in a traumatic situation, such as physical, emotional, or sexual abuse when you were young. These types of resentments will only be resolved by accepting they happened (remember acceptance is not the same as approval) and working toward forgiving a very sick perpetrator. I would suggest you make someone, with whom you can honestly confide, aware that you are undergoing this process, so you can check-in with them when you're not feeling great, which is bound to happen! Being honest, open-minded, and willing (H.O.W), is crucial to our ability to learn new behaviors. It takes time to form less desirable habits therefore it will also take you time to form more desirable habits. The key here is to be gentle with yourself. First acknowledge that this isn't an easy process and you will need support.

You cannot change over-night, but your moral inventory will help you to see exactly what you *do* need to change, so you can put a plan into action of *how* to change. Once you've conducted a thorough assessment of yourself, you are ready to share your findings with a trusted confidant (friend, teacher, counsellor, or spiritual advisor). Remember that your perspective on things is not always exactly as things are. It is necessary that you are open to guidance from other people about the best way to proceed in order to change, so you don't continue repeating harmful behavior patterns.

Not enough attention is given to the role of shame in the onset of mental health issues and subsequent addictions. Shame is an unpleasant, self-conscious emotion typically associated with a negative evaluation of the self, withdrawal motivations, and feelings of distress, exposure, mistrust, powerlessness, and worthlessness, which I believe is a fundamental component of The Spiritual Malady. Shame is a clear signal that our positive feelings have been interrupted, it informs us of an internal state of inadequacy, unworthiness, dishonor, regret, or disconnection. Another person or circumstance can trigger shame in us but also failure to meet our own ideals or standards can be a trigger. Given that shame can lead us to feel that our whole self is flawed, bad, or subject to exclusion, it motivates us to hide or to do something to save face. It's no wonder, therefore, that shame avoidance can lead to withdrawal from society (isolation), and to substance and/or behavioral addictions that attempt to mask its impact.

Shame is often confused with guilt; an emotion we might experience as a result of a wrongdoing about which we feel remorseful and wish to make amends. Though the terms 'shame' and 'guilt' are sometimes used interchangeably, most research on these emotions has found that they are distinct experiences. Guilt usually lasts for a brief time, whereas shame may be a core experience of the self. Whereas we are likely to admit our guilt, or talk to others about a situation that left us feeling guilty, it's much less likely that we'll broadcast our shame. In fact, we'll most likely conceal our shame because it doesn't make a distinction between an action and the self. With shame, 'bad' behavior is not separate from a 'bad' self, as it is with guilt.

Any situation, real or imagined, can trigger a shame response. For example, one might attack oneself for being inferior in competitive endeavors, or believe others will become aware of some concealed flaw. Shame will be felt when we anticipate being viewed as lacking (or inadequate) in our intellect, appearance, or abilities. For example, a woman who gained a lot of weight might have difficulty leaving her house because she wants to avoid the shame that is triggered by being out in public. She has devalued herself and her expectation is that others will judge her harshly. She knows that some people will judge her because she judges herself and others.

In order to escape shame's self-diminishing effects, expressing contempt toward another person or attacking them with a shaming comment re-locates one's own shame in the other. A man who anticipates being judged as inadequate, for example, might manipulate the self-esteem of his partner by degrading her. When she becomes weak, self-conscious, and needs his approval, he then becomes more confident, as well as able to blame her for any failure on his part. Relocating one's own shame in another person is a typical self-protective maneuver among narcissists, since at the core of narcissism is unbearable internalized shame that is denied consciousness. Needing to hide a devalued sense of self, narcissists can appear self-inflating or entitled and provoke envy in people around them, which is how I believe I often used to appear (and still can occasionally) before I started my recovery journey of change.

Shame is contagious and especially difficult – if not toxic for children – because it's an emotion that is concealed, especially by victims of aggression or abuse. The anticipation of being shamed by a parent or peer can create anxiety in a child. Shame can be experienced as such a negative, intense emotion of self-loathing that it can lead one to disown it, or, in the case of one who acts like a bully, give it away by evoking that emotion in others. Kids who bully and tease (like I did and had done to me) can easily figure out what makes other kids ashamed, and they are highly skilled at triggering the emotion of shame in their peers. Children are also subject to the transmission of shame when they are related to someone who is behaving shamefully. When children are emotionally or physically abandoned, abused, or neglected, they often take on the shame that belongs to the adult who left or hurt them by assuming that it's because they themselves are the 'bad' one. Some children, therefore, behave in ways that make them culpable for the shame that actually belongs to their parents.

Other causes of shame include: the stigmatization of certain sexual interactions, such as homosexual sex or sex between unmarried couples; self-esteem issues, as people with low self-esteem may struggle with feelings of shame even when they can point to no specific source of the shame; feeling shame for violating certain religious prescriptions; gaslighting (attempting to convince someone that their perceptions are wrong) can also lead to shame. Trauma from mental and physical abuse and childhood sexual abuse are also common causes of shame in adulthood – especially among adults who feel embarrassed about their abuse experiences.

For some people, feelings of shame may begin in childhood and continue well into adulthood. Some people may be conscious of such feelings whereas others may be unaware of their shame and hide it under behaviors such as anger, addiction, and/or narcissism, which is my story. Living with shame can be extremely painful and difficult, as it can prevent people from meeting their core needs, such as the maintenance of self-esteem, hope for the future, friendship, intimacy, productivity, and love. Some people even respond to shame by engaging in all manner of self-harm rituals, such as cutting, burning, and strangulation, and I would also postulate that tattoos (and piercings) might fall into the self-harm bracket. There is definitely an element of addiction to the pain, as the endorphins released in the brain during tattooing and piercing make the person feel good and cause a euphoric feeling. I have over forty individual tattoos all over my body, which might be considered an addiction by some people.

Studies of shame consistently find that it can play an integral role in suicide. People who feel guilt may have the ability to take-action to overcome their guilt but shame is much more difficult to overcome. Embarrassment, likewise, is often a transient state, but shame fundamentally affects a person's sense of self, potentially triggering or worsening suicidal thoughts. Addictions are the primary way in which most people suffering from shame attempt to nullify or medicate it, but the cycle of shame unfortunately continues exponentially, as the addiction progresses and the addict performs more and more shameful acts in their addiction. This is why Step Four (Made a searching and fearless moral inventory of ourselves) and Step Five (Admitted to God, to ourselves, and to another human being the exact nature of our wrongs) of The Twelve Step Program are life-savingly important to the recovering addict. The process of confession relieves the person of their guilt and shame and prevents them from blaming others – paving the way for forgiveness of others, and most importantly, forgiveness of self.

In openly admitting our faults, our guilt, and our shame, to another person and to our Higher Power, it deflates our ego. It's a very difficult part of the process of change but also necessary for peace of mind and contentment. Sharing your moral inventory is the beginning of true, honest, and humble relationships with other people. But how are you to choose the right person with whom to share your inventory? Pick a person you trust; someone who has been through similar life experiences and a similar process of confession is preferable (but not essential).

I think we all wish for the ability to relax in the company of others, and this is a matter of trust. Often, people only have one or two people whom they completely trust and feel relaxed with (usually their partner and/or best friend, or a parent or sibling), which means we don't feel 100% relaxed (in varying degrees) in the presence of others. If we lost trust in the person or persons with whom we had trust, this could render us anxious and restless in their presence also, which is a very uncomfortable place to be. This is why having a sponsor/mentor that you trust implicitly is so important in Twelve Step fellowships. The person you pick to share the findings from your moral inventory should be a person who is capable of listening, accepting you for who you are, and not passing judgment. You don't want to put yourself in a position to be emotionally harmed, as this would be counter-productive to what you're trying to achieve. The idea is to build trust by sharing openly and honestly with an individual who might well share back some of their relatable experiences, which helps with the unburdening of guilt and shame, as I can attest.

My experience of sharing my moral inventory with my first Twelve Step sponsor was a life-changing event. Immediately afterwards it felt like a huge weight had been lifted from my shoulders, and I was finally able to look myself in the eye (in the mirror) and acknowledge, without ego, that I'm not a bad person; I'm just a person with an illness trying to get well.

If you talk through every fear, every resentment, and every relationship issue one-by-one with your chosen confidant, by the end of the session you will likely feel some sense of relief, or it might just be an emotionally painful experience that requires some healing time afterwards. Before you finish, make sure you share any secrets you would rather not share. *Now* is the time to let it all out. Be brave and do not hold back. Peace of mind and contentment rests on a clear conscience. It's imperative that you don't walk away with any secrets that might later cause you emotional distress, as this might be the catalyst for emotional disorder and mental illness to arise in the future. I know of many men and women whose secrets have sent them to an early grave. We are only as, "sick as our secrets," as they say in The Rooms.

Your ego is essentially the enduring and conscious element of 'You' that accumulates all your experiences, and it is the mediator between your primitive drives and the demands of your social and physical environment, comprising your sense of self-esteem and self-importance. Your ego (the veil/interface) keeps you trapped between the past (depression) and the future (anxiety), which keeps you out of the present (peace) where your true essence (Consciousness) resides. Remember, there is only ever *now*. The future does not exist, as every future moment you are going to experience is a series of now moments, and the past (also a series of now moments) has gone – existing only as memories that your ego uses to distract you from the now (where your ego cannot function or be In control).

Your ego might feel 'bruised' or 'deflated' following the 'confession experience,' as the ego is strengthened by those selfish, self-centered, fearful behaviors that keep you feeling superior or 'less than' other people. Continuous ego-deflation through the process of taking regular moral inventory will lead to greater humility and a feeling of 'oneness' with humanity and the universe at large, which I experience regularly as a result of continuing this practice.

There's no getting away from the fact that confession can be an emotionally painful process but pain is the touchstone of emotional/spiritual development and the facilitator to peace of mind and contentment. The process of sharing your moral inventory, fearlessly and thoroughly, is a spring-board toward an eventual spiritual awakening, which, once achieved, is well worth any emotional discomfort experienced along the way. This is why the wise and spiritually enlightened consider suffering to be Grace, as conscious-awareness arises from pain.

Spiritual awakening, in my experience, is a grace-filled gift that has to be acquired through hard work. It can't simply be given from one person to another. It can't be bought, it can't be stolen, and it can't be explained either. It can only be experienced, and everyone's experience is their own affair, but the common denominator is a phenomenal psychic change, which brings about a revolution in one's perception of the world coupled with peace of mind and contentment.

"BE THE CHANGE THAT YOU WISH TO
SEE IN THE WORLD"

– Mahatma Gandhi (Leader of the Indian independence
movement)

LESSON SIX: CHANGE

Following your confession experience, you will have a list of shortcomings from your moral inventory; selfish, self-seeking, dishonest, and fearful behaviors, such as: anger, cowardice, self-pity, self-justification, self-importance/egotism, self-condemnation, lying/evasiveness, impatience, intolerance, false pride, jealousy, envy, apathy, procrastination, insincerity, gossip, and greed. In order to change, you must be willing to place emphasis on overcoming these behaviors that have a negative effect on inter-personal relationships by asking for help from your fellows, and your Higher Power. Before attempting this, ask yourself, how motivated are you to develop emotionally and spiritually, to change and grow in a positive direction, and, to better yourself?

You will be released from the bondage of every one of your less desirable qualities, if you truly wish for it to happen and if you work for it. With a real willingness to share your issues, coupled with the power of meaningful prayer and meditation, you can ask for these obstacles to be removed, so that you might become the best version of yourself and ultimately more helpful to others. My experience has been, and continues to be, my Higher Power helps me change, but only if I have faith that it can happen. Without faith nothing changes. Aside from faith in my Higher Power, the three things that continue to be essential to my personal evolution are:

- Spending time with like-minded people (who are interested in change)
- Putting time aside every day for my spiritual practices (prayer, meditation, readings, and walking my dog)

- Living my life with humility rather than ego (being of service to others as often as possible)

Having analyzed your less desirable qualities, now would be a good time to write down a list of all your more desirable attributes. Write down at least ten to start with, then add to this list as time goes by. For example: I am honest, loving, kind, affectionate, thoughtful, sincere, complimentary, hard-working, passionate, and faithful. Write down examples of when you have exhibited these traits. You'll find that you have as many – if not more – desirable attributes to practice and build upon that will improve your inter-personal relationships moving forward.

We are all born with natural instincts to eat, build relationships, attain status, and to be safe and secure. Providing you don't exceed these natural drives you will likely enjoy peace of mind and live a happy and fulfilled life. It's quite as simple as that, but it's not an easy path to walk. To make progress in the building of your character, first you must be willing to let go of the powerful desire for validation in order to transcend often childish and overwhelming cravings for more success and ever-more pleasurable experiences and material satisfactions. As the great and influential German philosopher Immanuel Kant said, "Enlightenment is man's emergence from his self-imposed immaturity." I don't believe the desire for more 'stuff' will ever completely leave us – unless we practice renunciation and attain spiritual Enlightenment. This work is more about evolving the ability to pause and choose rather than mindlessly acting and consuming.

In the Buddhist view, pain is inevitable whereas suffering is a choice, which has been my experience thus far in recovery. I think a common misconception is that people who become 'Enlightened' simply stop changing and growing, and stop working on themselves. I would argue, however, if you idle in a retrogressive groove once you've reached the pinnacle of transcendence, you might still slide back toward a troubled cognizance and emotional disorder. One must continue to evolve by engaging in spiritual practices and being of service to others. Sitting 'blissed-out' in a cave in the Himalayas is no good to anyone but yourself. I would also speculate that 'Enlightenment' is a state that cannot be maintained. Rather, it is an experience that one has, which the enlightened person uses as a springboard to help others achieve the same goal, like Guatama Buddha did over 2500 years ago.

German author and spiritual teacher, Eckhart Tolle notably documented his instantaneous 'awakening' in 1977 in his book, *The Power of Now*, "For many years I had been deeply identified with thinking and the painful, heavy emotions that had accumulated inside. My thought activity was mostly negative, and my sense of identity was also mostly negative, although I tried hard to prove to myself and to the world that I was good enough by working very hard academically. But even after I had achieved academic success, I was happy for two weeks or three and then the depression and anxiety came back. On that night there was a disidentification from this unpleasant dream of thinking and the painful emotions. The nightmare became unbearable and that triggered the separation of consciousness from its identification with form. I woke up and suddenly realized myself as the I Am and that was deeply peaceful. The next morning, everything was beautiful and intensively alive." For me, Tolle is clearly describing the distinction between Consciousness, which he refers to as the "I Am," and his ego-mind, which he refers to as, "the unpleasant dream of thinking." Having read all of Tolle's books and listened to him extensively on various podcasts, he claims to no longer be identified with the ego-mind, which means he has attained peace from mind and may well be considered self-actualized or Enlightened.

Tolle spent many years meditating and reading extensively in spiritual and psychoanalytic literature, as well as poetry and mythology, before he was later recognized as a spiritual teacher or Buddha-like figure. I believe every human being is a potential

'Buddha,' with the capacity for Enlightenment and unconditional love, and therefore responding rather than reacting to life. It is the ego-mind that prevents this from happening, as its identification with form and social conditioning creates false needs and an illusory sense of identity and separation that, in reality, is nothing but a barrier of dreams, fantasies, and illusions.

At the Vipassana retreat, S.N Goenka's lectures on the teachings of Gautama Buddha were concerned with reaching ultimate Enlightenment. I am more concerned with helping people to become 'conscious' and learn how to cope with (and overcome) life's most difficult experiences, such as bereavement, mental health issues, relationship breakdowns, and chronic addiction, as Enlightenment seems unattainable for most people – including myself. Often, a person's children have to carry on the process of change that he/she started, as one lifetime isn't enough. Hopefully, Alice, Isobel, or Lillian might carry on the work I have started, which was to acknowledge, accept, and progressively learn to feel the collective pain of my family, so my children and their children can accept and feel the inevitable pains of life rather than avoiding them or numbing them like I, and previous generations, did. If we can simply learn to cope with life – on life's terms rather than our own terms – by gradually dis-identifying with the ego, I believe we can experience peace of mind and contentment (the majority of the time), and enjoy lasting happiness, then pass this learning on to our children, so they don't have to live an ego-dominated life.

The human ego is essentially a mechanism for survival, replicating behavioral strategies that have proven successful in the past and projecting how these strategies might prove successful in the future. The ego's appeal to the past and projection to the future, however, deprives human beings of the ability to live authentically in the present – causing them to repress genuine emotions and to shut themselves off from joyful experiences that arise naturally in the present moment. The result is that people poison themselves with all manner of neuroses, jealousies, insecurities, and substances – born out of the ego's constant flitting from past to future – and back again – in a continuous cycle.

Psychological repression, as a result of keeping shameful experiences locked away in the past, makes suppressed feelings re-emerge in other guises; often obsessive-compulsive behaviors. Sexual repression, for example, results in society's obsession with porn and sex. Instead of suppressing, I believe people must learn to accept themselves unconditionally, so they can live with themselves in the present, while simultaneously recognizing the behaviors that cause them (and others) to suffer, in order to change them. This cannot merely be an intellectual exercise, as the mind will simply assimilate it as one more piece of information that it may or may not make use of, or disregard. Self-awareness (intuition) and action is needed.

Although reason is what sets us apart from all the other creatures in the world, reason has no place here, as reason is what often gets us into trouble in the first place. I can give a million reasons why something is a good idea, when clearly it isn't from everyone else's perspective. Don't get me wrong, I'm not an anti-intellectual, as I believe intellect and reason have their place. Reason and intellect will essentially help you to educate yourself, get a job, achieve success, engage in relationships, and, crucially, "become somebody in the world before you can (transcend intellect and reason) and become nobody," to quote spiritual teacher Ram Dass. For me, intuition, which speaks from the heart-mind (in Buddhist philosophy) and is far more spacious and aware, trumps reason, which speaks from the ego-mind.

To emphasize my point, it is written in the 'Big Book' *Alcoholics Anonymous*, "Logic is great stuff. We liked it. We still like it. It is not by chance we were given the power to reason, to examine the evidence of our senses, and to draw conclusions. That is one of man's magnificent attributes. We agnostically inclined would not feel satisfied with a proposal which does not lend itself to reasonable approach and interpretation. Hence we are at pains to tell why we think our present faith is reasonable, why we think it more sane and logical to believe than not to believe, why we say our former thinking was soft and mushy when we threw up our hands in doubt and said, we don't know. When we became alcoholics, crushed by a self-imposed crisis we could not postpone or evade, we had to fearlessly face the proposition that either God is everything or else He is nothing. God either is, or He isn't. What was our choice to be?... Arrived at this point, we were squarely confronted with the question of faith. We couldn't duck the issue... We were grateful that reason had brought us so far. But somehow, we couldn't quite step ashore. Perhaps we had been leaning too heavily on reason that last mile and we did not like to lose our support."

Even if you're a tough-minded atheistic sceptic, who believes only in unbiased science – in evidence and evidence alone – you must still know that one day many of the things you believe will be replaced by better science. Experimental science continually improves upon itself therefore 'truth' is not necessarily 'truth' but the best belief considering the current evidence. We all adjust our beliefs accordingly, as science changes, to believe in the most useful belief at any given time. Christopher Columbus, who changed the Earth to a globe from flat, is the most obvious example I can think of, as prior to this, the 'truth' was: the Earth is flat. Scientific truth is not a noun but an adjective describing experiences. The ultimate 'Truth,' however, has to be Enlightenment, as to become a 'Buddha' (an Enlightened One) means to transcend reason, logic, and intellect, clearing away all indecision and confusion to experience reality *as it is*.

To bypass reason, meditation is needed, so you can become aligned with 'intuition' that I believe is Consciousness, which guides you toward empathy and compassion – away from egoic reactions that are grounded in fear. For example, when you feel that you are being criticized, your ego-alarm is activated, which you experience as tension, wincing, anxiety, or panic. Within seconds your ego-defense kicks-in, and it can implore you to react to the perceived criticism with an attack of its own. The trick is to learn to acknowledge the ego-alarm with conscious-awareness and metaphorically step back from it, so you can objectively observe the emotions that arise – before your ego-mind creates a narrative. This is a difficult skill to learn and takes diligent meditative practice, but as your self-awareness increases, you'll develop the ability to detect the ego-alarm and not react to it. Eventually, with conscious awareness, you will learn to pause (as Consciousness is in the pause) and disable the alarm completely by lovingly replacing your egoic reactions with compassionate responses.

I think most of us can admit to liking the feeling of dominance and control over others, or allowing greed to masquerade as ambition. Self-righteous anger can also be enjoyable. Gossip and criticism can bring a quiet satisfaction that, again, affords a comfortable sense of superiority. Procrastination, sloth, and gluttony, are milder character traits that we might want to cling on to, yet these attributes hinder our progress if we are aiming for spiritual betterment. Overcoming certain traits that you currently wish to hold on to might take time but remain open-minded to the ideal of letting go of your 'baggage' and allowing your Higher Power to take it from you. As a result of letting go, I'm no longer searching for extremes. I'm not a thrill seeker like I used to be, so I don't enjoy great highs and the inevitable deep lows that follow. I'm much more comfortable with the middle-way, mediocrity, and even the mundane, because I understand that if I'm happy with life's mundanity, I'm rarely unhappy.

If you aim for emotional balance as the ultimate destination that you know you might never reach, you can simply let go, relax, and enjoy the journey, as you accumulatively experience more and more contentment with an ever-evolving peace of mind. According to ascended master Levi H. Dowling, Jesus Christ said, "He who obeys the laws, maintains an equilibrium in all his parts, thus insures true harmony; and harmony is health, while discord is disease. That which produces harmony in all parts of man is medicine insuring health."

We are not aiming for perfection because this creates perfectionism, which is an illness in itself. I suffered greatly from perfectionism until 2019 when, following a conversation with my sponsor about how my perfectionism was preventing self-acceptance, I dropped the nagging desire to be perfect in favor of accepting myself, *as I am*, which increased my level of serenity as a by-product. Serenity is the eventual fruit of continued spiritual practices and principles, but, as already highlighted, serenity is unattainable without some measure of humility. The humbler you become, the more peace of mind you will experience, and the more happiness you will enjoy. In a world where power and riches seem to be the chief aims in life for so many, humility will seem like a counter-intuitive goal to aim toward, yet people who have experienced complete material, emotional, and mental ruin, before regaining some level of contentment, will attest that character-building and spiritual values must come before material achievement.

I had to lose pretty much every aspect of my old life, including my job, my marriage, my friends, and my material possessions, before I was humbled. A defining moment on my continual journey toward an ever-increasing humility was a trip to India in 2011 – two years into my sobriety. Experiencing India's poverty led to me giving away all my material possessions that I did not need, and I have since adopted a yearly housecleaning – sending bags full to the charity shops. The catalyst for that experience happened in Thailand in 2009 when I was newly sober. The unwanted attention my TAG Heuer watch gained from the indigenous folk left me feeling slightly gross. I could see how they thought that one material possession would make them happy if only they could afford it. The truth is, the watch brought me fleeting happiness when I first bought it, as I wasn't happy with myself at the time, so my misery continued despite having an expensive and beautifully crafted time-piece on my wrist. I sold it not long after I arrived back in the UK, and I have never missed it since.

Material achievement without humble foundations will inevitably and eventually bring about spiritual and emotional bankruptcy. Material pleasures are short-lived and they do not equate to contentment or lasting happiness. Buying the latest pair of fashionable shoes, for example, will provide you with a momentary dopamine hit – a quick 'happiness fix' – but inevitably it fades and you are always left wanting more. This is the same with every material pleasure. In the past, I've spent thousands of pounds on watches, coats, shoes, and other material satisfactions, but none of them brought me lasting happiness. Conversely, being of continual service to others, with no thought of praise or reward, gives me a quiet satisfaction that is simply priceless, as it *does* bring me peace of mind and a contentment that lasts.

Following your 'confession experience,' you should now be ready and willing to try the way of humility by seeking the removal of your character defects in much the same way as humbly admitting that you are powerless over people, places, and things – and that your Higher Power will do for you what you cannot do for yourself. Humility is a necessity if you want to experience true freedom. It is the nourishing ingredient that gives rise to serenity. A change in attitude, from wanting to achieve happiness by acquiring more material satisfactions, will lead to you being gifted happiness as a by-product of selfless action. The poignant question is: how can we change our materialistic attitude that is so ingrained in our consumer-driven society? The answer: one only has to ask your Higher Power for help. It's all a matter of intention. If you pray for the willingness to change, gradually you *will* change. This is a suggested daily prayer that might help you progressively make that change:

Higher Power,
I'm humbly asking that you take all of me, good and bad,
please remove from me every single defect of character,
which stand in the way of my usefulness to you and my fellows,
give me strength, as I go out from here, to do your will.

Helpful acts have a positive pay-off. If you wish to feel better about yourself and about life in general, do more things for other people. By thinking of others, you will concentrate less on your own perceived problems and, as a result, life will become less stressful and more enjoyable. Also, experiencing another person's happiness as a result of your help will make you feel good. Your self-esteem will rise and your confidence will increase, as will your level of humility.

"Be honest and love everyone," said mystical Hindu guru Neem Karoli Baba to his disciple Ram Dass (formerly Harvard clinical psychology professor Richard Alpert). Complete honesty with everyone at all times is difficult enough, but to love everyone, even those you don't know and those you dislike, is an alien proposition to most. To be honest and to love everyone is to be a servant of mankind, which is exactly what Richard Alpert became, as Ram Dass means 'Servant of God' in Hindi. Serving other people serves you because the irony is that by helping people you help yourself. "Research has shown that a simple act of kindness directed towards another improves the functioning of the immune system and stimulates the production of serotonin in both the recipient of the kindness and the person extending the kindness," said American philosopher, self-help author, and motivational speaker Dr. Wayne Dyer.

Altruism is essentially a type of pro-social behavior intended to benefit another individual or group of individuals by sharing, comforting, rescuing, or generally helping. Altruism (selflessness) is the opposite of egoism (selfishness) and is carried out with no expectation of external or internal reward. Altruism is central to the teachings of Jesus found in *The Bible*, especially in *The Sermon on the Mount* and *The Sermon on the Plain*. In Islam, the concept 'īthār' (إيثار) is the notion of 'preferring others to oneself.' For Sufi's (Islamic mystics), this means devotion to others through complete forgetfulness of one's own concerns. Altruism also figures prominently in Buddhism; love and compassion are components of all forms of Buddhist Dharma with the focus on treating all sentient beings as equals. Love is the wish that all beings be happy and compassion is the wish that all beings be free from suffering.

To become altruistic, therefore, you must be willing to take action and work hard on yourself in order to change, but before you can truly help others you must first learn to forgive others and most importantly, forgive yourself.

"I WANT TO TRY MAKING THINGS RIGHT
BECAUSE PICKING UP THE PIECES IS WAY
BETTER THAN LEAVING THEM
THE WAY THEY ARE"

– Simone Elkeles (American bestselling author)

LESSON SEVEN: ATONEMENT

Your moral inventory presents you with a list of people whom you've had resentments toward. Paradoxically, you might owe them an apology. Add to that list all the people to whom you've caused emotional, mental, or physical harm, then become willing to make amends to *all of them*. This is where true freedom and peace of mind is born, from forgiveness. Amends might come in the form of a written or verbal apology, or it may be a case of leaving a person to get on with their life without interruption from you (as is the case with my ex-wife). Your spiritual advisor, teacher, or trusted friend, will help you make those decisions, deterring you from any amends that might harm the other person. It's not productive to focus on the wrongs people have done to you, so instead, concentrate only on how you have wronged them. It's easy to triumphantly point out another person's misbehavior, and minimize or completely forget about your own shortcomings, but this would be counter-productive in your quest for humility, which, don't forget, is a pre-requisite to achieving peace of mind.

Forgiveness is key when it comes to humbling oneself; it's a powerful and affirmative part of our humanity. Everyone has something they wish to be forgiven for and someone they need to forgive. The healing power of forgiveness allows you to truly move on. A life lived without forgiveness is a life of emotional discomfort, as I well know having lived with resentments for many years prior to recovery. Not forgiving people *hurts you not them*, as the burden of resentment creates dis-ease within you, which, over time, demands alleviation. This is why resentment is deemed the 'number one offender' in Twelve Step fellowships, as it not only drives destructive behaviors, such as angry outbursts and jealous or envious snipes, but many an alcoholic/addict has drank/used themselves to death over a resentment because resentment exacerbates emotional disorder and mental illness.

Forgiveness is ultimately a gift to yourself, as it allows your wounds to heal. Once I forgave people who I felt had wronged me, and forgave myself for the harm I caused others, I was free at last. You can forgive your parents for their blindness and denial, your siblings for their temerity, your friends for their selfishness, and yourself for your own ignorance – and for continually succumbing to your desires and your aversions. Reconcile the past and accept life *as it is* right now. Freedom will come in an instant when you truly let go of the past by sharing it in a safe environment, feel the emotions, then let them go forever.

I'm quite a forgiving person because I grew up in a household where we argued a lot, and were often mean to each other, but as soon as we apologized all was forgiven. However, continuing this behavior has caused me lots of issues in relationships because everyone grows up in different types of environments. What you live with you learn, what you learn you practice, what you practice you become, and what you become has consequences. Through working the Family of Origin Program designed by counsellor, author, and lecturer Earnie Larsen (who was a pioneer in the field of recovery from addictive behaviors and the originator of the process known as 'Stage 2 Recovery,' whereby people develop maturity and emotional sobriety), I was able to identify that, as a result of my early upbringing and environment, I learned how to be affectionate, loving, and kind from my parents. They also instilled a sense in me that I could be whatever I wanted to be and that they would always support me no matter what. However, I also learned to steal and lie; to scream and shout and dominate; if someone hurts me, punish them or sulk. I learned that I must look perfect to the outside world when inside I don't feel ok; if I play the martyr and sulk I get what I want; I can use substances (including food) to avoid reality and responsibility, and to 'achieve' in order to feel alive and worthwhile. These messages were unwittingly passed down to me by my family and friends, who had the same messages passed down to them.

As a result of these learned behaviors, I practiced using food and drugs (including alcohol) to avoid dealing with my feelings and avoid responsibilities; I pretended to be perfect – rarely being vulnerable and honest about the way I felt; I used manipulation, control, aggression, and anger, to get my own way; I used silent scorn and sulks to get my own way; I used martyrdom and self-pity to get my own way; I dominated most of the men in my life and used most women for sexual gratification, and I over-worked and over-exercised to make me feel ok. As a result of this behavior, I became a 'double-minded' man (always questioning myself); an alcoholic and a workaholic; a perfectionist who felt like a failure; lonely, depressed, and isolated; an adult-child shirking responsibilities; I manipulated and controlled people; I didn't have many close male friends and I flitted from one sexual relationship to another with women – rarely getting close to anyone; I dominated my partners, and I was often selfish and self-piteous.

Seeing all this in black and white wasn't easy, in fact it was really painful, and it clearly wasn't something I was going to put right overnight. It takes courage, patience, and tolerance to do this work. It was worthwhile, however, because it enabled me to change and become a better man. Since completing the Family of Origin Program with my sponsor in March 2018, I'm progressively becoming more-loving and kind, less selfish, and more vulnerable by being more honest. Examples of my recovery are: responsible engagement and future planning with Adele; my unconditionally loving relationships with my daughter Alice, my step-children Lillian and Isobel, and my dog Teddy; my honest and less reliant relationship with my parents, and my responsible job as a Team Leader. I'm also more decisive; I'm less controlling and manipulative; I rarely express anger by shouting and I can express myself calmly; I admit my faults and apologize when I need to; I'm hardly ever anxious; I don't suffer from depression; I'm less interested in material satisfactions; I trust people more, and I don't owe anyone an apology today.

When thinking about making amends, first ask yourself, have you ever lied or cheated? Have you ever been irresponsible, cold, irritable, impatient, critical, or humorless? Have you ever neglected others? Have you ever tried to dominate or control people? Have you ever been self-piteous or depressive without cause? Of-course you have! Ransack your memory and get it all down on paper, then ask yourself whom have you harmed, and in what way? Are you willing to make amends now, in the future, or never? How do you plan to make amends?

Wherever possible, a face-to-face apology is preferable; written apologies hold nothing like the weight of a humble face-to-face encounter. Unlike a written apology, the tone of sincerity cannot be misinterpreted if a face-to-face amend is executed appropriately.

Some people never forgive, remaining victims forever. Not just a victim of the insult or injury but also to an identification with their wound that may impact future relationships and their own sense of identity. The initial harm can become a never-ending injury like Post Traumatic Stress Disorder. PTSD is intense psychic damage caused by recurrent victimhood, but you don't have to have PTSD to get stuck in resentments from the past. Forgive whenever you can, grieve when necessary, and remember what is needed to learn from resentment-fueled experiences, as victimhood doesn't help you in the long run. Perhaps the most positive perspective and appropriate response to harm caused by others is to accept and be grateful that you have survived unpleasant or even traumatic experiences.

Forgiveness is about putting the past in its place, letting go with an affirmative change in your heart, and living in the present. It has a power worth exploring again and again because forgiveness and making amends brings us closer to people. The best example I have of this was 'falling out' with one of my best friends

Jonathan in 2009 and not speaking to him for around five years. When I eventually looked at my part in the resentment, I was able to forgive myself for my childishness and prideful hubris, and forgive Jonathan for the way I deemed he had wronged me before making amends by admitting my wrong-doing. As a result, I was present at his wedding in 2017 and he will be one of my two best men at my wedding in July 2020. We are closer now than ever before.

After making your immediate amends and enjoying the sense of relief that comes with those apologies, you might be tempted to rest on your laurels and consider putting off, or skipping, the most dreaded and potentially humiliating amends. You might even manufacture plausible excuses for avoiding these issues entirely, or you might procrastinate – convincing yourself the time isn't right when you've already passed up numerous opportunities to right a particular wrong. Some sceptical and even difficult receptions from people might discourage you and make you pessimistic but if you're well prepared, such reactions won't deter you from persevering. I've had a number of sceptical receptions to amends over the years but I've managed to win over the scepticism by remaining steadfast with my improved behavior. Approval and praise might also tip you off balance toward egotism but there are sure to be less pleasant reactions that will balance things out!

Financial amends to businesses (e.g. for stolen goods) shouldn't be avoided. I had to pay back three sums of money to organizations I'd stolen from in the past, which I found really difficult because I'd become financially insecure even though I had plenty of money. Once I paid all the money back, however, I found myself free from financial insecurity, as both the physical and emotional sense of debt had been quashed. Although there's a fair amount of shame and embarrassment involved in these types of amends, it's essential that you are fearless and thorough in every step of your journey – admitting the damage you've done and making a sincere apology. Financial amends go a long way to evolving humility. Generous responses from most of your creditors to such sincerity might astonish you, as it did with me. Even your severest and most justified critics will often go easy on you in response to your honesty, which I experienced when my creditors didn't contact the police even though they could have done so.

Before making an amend, pause and ask your Higher Power for guidance. You should also run your amends, each and every one, by your trusted friend, mentor, teacher, sponsor, or spiritual advisor. This way, you'll be less likely to cause any harm to the people to whom you are making amends, or to yourself. The only exception to making direct amends will be in cases where your confession might cause harm to that person or other people. You shouldn't, for example, disclose details of your behavior to your parents, which might distress them and displace their peace of mind. Prolonged amends will often be more effective than one-off amends following dramatic revelations. Above all, you should have a complete willingness to make amends as fast and as far as possible, and be absolutely sure that you are not delaying because you are afraid. Be ready to take *full* responsibility for your past actions and simultaneously commit to maintaining the wellbeing of others.

Trusting that the amends process will be beneficial to you and the recipient, then having your trust rewarded, builds faith in your Higher Power, as you see that the process works. The sooner you begin the amends process, the more presently you will experience peace of mind and contentment. If you are painstaking about this phase of your spiritual development, you'll be amazed to find that you experience a newfound freedom and happiness. You won't regret the past nor wish to shut the door on it. You'll comprehend the word serenity and you will know real peace of mind. No matter how much your past actions have caused suffering, you'll see how your experiences can actually benefit others. Any feelings of uselessness or self-pity will disappear. You'll lose interest in selfish things and gain interest in your fellows. Self-seeking will slip away and your whole attitude and outlook upon life will change. Fear of people and of economic insecurity will leave you and you will intuitively know how to handle situations that used to baffle you. You'll suddenly realize that your Higher Power is doing for you what you could not do for yourself, but these promises will *only* materialize *if you work for them*.

I met my friend Matthew when I moved from London to Birmingham in 2017. He was born in 1936 – one year after Alcoholics Anonymous was founded in Akron, Ohio, United States – and he has been in recovery from alcoholism (and addiction to prescribed medication) since November 1984. This is his story in relation to atonement...

I shall be forever grateful for The Twelve Step Program of A.A, but in particular for the 9th Step (that states: Made direct amends to such people wherever possible except when to do so would injure them or others), which enabled me to feel comfortable in a world to which I had previously felt I didn't belong. I had so wanted to feel part of a group, class or team but always felt on the outside. It was as if I was perpetually watching a video of life but unable to step through the screen and participate. The 9th Step changed all that.

I believe the key to the success of this step for me, lay partially in the attempted thoroughness with which I took the 8th Step. This was the first time in my life I had 'stepped into someone else's shoes' to try to understand what it must have felt like to have me harm them in some way. Thus, when making amends, I was able to be quite specific about what actions/attitudes I was trying to make amends for. I believe this approach was more effective than general 'blanket' apologies.

When I came to A.A the very first emotions which surfaced after only two or three meetings were remorse and guilt. This was in connection with the way I had treated my ex-wife and two daughters. I quickly perceived that I had been a failure both as a husband and a father. During the last 5 years of my drinking I had tried to rule the household with a rod of iron and had subjected all three to mental abuse and neglect. I was physically violent and there had been incidents involving a shotgun and attempted arson. I had become a thoroughly nasty piece of work. I had also conducted two high profile affairs without any regard for the resulting humiliation felt by my family.

The three of them were forced to go into hiding during the final stages of the marriage which eventually ended in divorce. Experienced A.A members tried to assure me that if I followed The Twelve Step Program to the best of my ability, I would find self-forgiveness and peace; that I was not a bad person trying to become a good person, but more a sick person trying to get better.

Within the first few weeks I decided to write a letter to each of them. I apologized in a general way for having been a failure as a husband and father. I have to admit that my motivation for writing the letters was to relieve myself of some of the guilt. This worked even though predictably I never received any reply.

After a few months I was able to be much more specific about the damage I had done to these three and I contacted my ex-wife and asked her if I could visit her for half an hour. I said a prayer before I went and asked God to help me in my mission. I expressed genuine regret for my failure as a husband and partner and went into some detail regarding the areas of failure. To give her credit, she heard me out but said very little. Despite having no reaction from her, I felt a great relief. Sadly, to this day, she wants nothing to do with me and told me I would not be welcome in her house again.

Shortly after this I moved to Wales to work on a caravan site and I invited my daughters to come and stay with me, one at a time. The first morning I took them breakfast in bed and asked each of them if they would be good enough to listen to me for half an hour. I then made as thorough amends as I could and once again experienced a great relief. When I had finished making verbal amends to my younger daughter she said, "I hear everything you say Dad, but you haven't mentioned the one thing which used to hurt us the most." When I asked her what this was she replied,

"When we used to get in from school all we wanted to do was to tell you how our day had gone but you never wanted to listen – all you wanted was to talk about yourself. You were never available." I owe her a great deal of thanks because for the first time in my life, as the result of what she said I started to really listen to other people – most especially in A.A meetings. I mean listening from the center of me – not with a view to how I'm going to reply or from any other egotistical perspective, but just listening with my ego on the back burner.

The outcome of commencement of amends to my daughters has been that I have the most wonderful relationship with one of them, but unfortunately not with the other, whom I have not seen now for well over ten years. She – like her mother – is unable to forgive me and this has to be her problem. From time to time I make attempts to build bridges and I continue to send cards for her birthday and Christmas.

I was twenty years old when my father died at the age of fifty-six. He was fundamentally a good man but was given to bouts of depression and outbursts of uncontrollable temper. He served as an officer in the army during the war and as a qualified industrial chemist, was involved in secret work relating to chemical warfare, or rather defense against it. I only saw him twice during this period and was nine years old when he returned home. He produced a rhinoceros hide whip with which he used to beat me whenever I stepped 'out of line.' I was naturally frightened of him. On the plus side he passed onto me a love of the countryside and taught me to fish and watch birds and to appreciate nature generally. These are priceless assets to this day.

From the age of sixteen I no longer wanted to be with him. I had discovered alcohol and the life-style which went with it. I stopped going out into the countryside with him and helping him in the garden. I was with him in the hospital at the end of his life and have to admit that I felt nothing except a kind of relief. He would no longer be around to disapprove of me.

When it came to making amends to my father my sponsor suggested that I write some notes about my shortcomings in the relationship and that I should pray for him and ask for his forgiveness. One evening I settled myself comfortably in a chair and was about to commence to pray when he appeared in front of me within a beautiful framework of tiny sparkling stars. He looked completely at peace. I wasn't at all frightened and I spoke aloud to him apologizing in so many words for my part in the decline of our relationship. He replied saying that at times he had not been the father I deserved. I couldn't say how long this encounter lasted but we made complete peace with one another.

My spiritual advisor told me afterwards that his appearance was a great gift to me and that it required an enormous effort for people who had passed back into spirit, to appear in this way. It required much assistance from their guides because it was necessary to lower their vibrations to a such a degree as would facilitate such an occurrence. He also said that it would never happen again. I love my father so much these days and because of the self-examination I have made, I have come to a complete understanding of him and his various personal demons.

The relationship with my Mother was the most influential in my life. She was a beautiful woman whom men adored but a complete narcissist. She bullied me and played strange games which involved making me jump and frightening me. With my father away in the army, I was obviously dependent on her completely. I remember that at the age of around three or four, she would sometimes put on her coat and hat, pick up a suitcase and say she was going to leave me. She would lock me in the house, walk down the path and out of sight. I was terrified of her.

I spent the rest of my life desperately trying to get her approval and love. To recount the story of my relationship with her would fill a book. This relationship influenced not only the way I felt about women but also men. She continued to abuse me in adulthood and I came to see that making amends to her was not only identifying my part in the dysfunctional aspect of the relationship but also stopping the abuse. It took me ten years in recovery to finally get the courage to deal with the abuse. The process was frightening but rewarding. She lived another three years after this and by this time we reached a stage where we could give each other a hug and say that we loved each other. For two very sick and emotionally disturbed people, this was a massive achievement.

Twenty-two years have passed since her death and I can honestly say that I have completely forgiven this woman and our relationship has grown beyond my hopes. I can now see that she was the greatest teacher I ever had, and I look forward to seeing her again when my time here is up.

My brother was born when I was six years old. His arrival was bad news for me especially when my mother seemed to idolize him and fuss over him to a degree which had been denied me. I therefore bullied him and teased him unmercifully. My treatment was finally too much for him to bear and one day he lost his temper and went for me with an axe. I've no doubt that had he caught up with me, he would have done some serious damage. It wasn't rocket science to identify how I had damaged him, and making amends has been rewarding for the both of us. We each feel we have the brother we deserve.

There were two local women with whom I had affairs. One of them was married and another had been in a long-term relationship. I made comprehensive apologies to them for treating them badly and for having introduced chaos into their lives. They both forgave me. I also made similar amends to the long-term partner of one of them who had threatened suicide when he discovered what had been going on. I hadn't intended to face him as I thought this fell into the category "…… where to do so would injure them or others." I was obviously quite wrong as he was unavoidably put in my path one day, and I knew immediately that this was God's planning and that I had to face him. After I had apologized, he held out his hand and shook mine in an act of forgiveness. A wonderful feeling.

I was once party to an insurance fraud in collusion with another person. The sum was quite substantial at that time. It was pointed out to me that if I made amends it would necessarily incriminate the other party, and that I had no right to do this. I have found an altruistic way of dealing with this which is proving appropriate.

There were many decent friends I once had, whom I simply stopped having contact with. I had begun to feel increasingly inadequate in their company. I contacted all of them and one of the amends brought about a life changing result. This particular friend was not only a very good London lawyer, but also a talented pianist who used to do the odd gig down there. I phoned him one day and explained how sorry I was that I had not been in touch. He was delighted to hear me and asked me if I was free the next Friday to play the piano for a party at the Danish Embassy. He had been booked to do it but something had cropped up and he was no longer available. I not only did the job for him but it gave me so much confidence that I auditioned for a London agent and got a wonderful six-month contract playing at a newly opened highly prestigious brasserie in Soho. I went on to play in several top venues over the next couple of years and I have since enjoyed a successful sideline as an events pianist. I have been grateful to have performed in many venues in Europe, the US and Egypt – as well as in several prestigious venues in London.

I was one of two drunks in my local village. In the final stages of my drinking, I was deeply ashamed of the person I was becoming and it was clear that people in the village were fed up with my antics. I had become completely isolated in my own sad world. After a few years in recovery I was approached by the local church elders to see if I would be willing to give a concert in the church to be billed as "An Evening With ………" Amazingly it seemed as though the whole village turned out – the church was packed. To this day I believe that everyone simply wanted to see me fall off the piano stool!! The evening was a success – the church made about £800 and so my amends to the community were made. I can walk down my own village street these days looking fellow villagers in the eye and not down at the pavement.

There were many more damaged people on my list. During the last years of my drinking, anyone who came into contact with me ran the risk of being damaged in some way. Where possible I have approached all these people. Two or three of them were unable to forgive me and I had to accept that. The problem then became theirs.

To summarize, I'm forever grateful for the extraordinary power of the 9th Step. The significance of the word 'painstaking' has never been lost on me and the Twelve Promises have come about in abundance in my life. They manifest themselves to some degree each day. I have been granted the true peace for which I was always searching. Thus, atonement has played an important part in this wonderful gift from a loving God.

Matthew D

"EQUANIMITY IS THE HALLMARK
OF SPIRITUALITY.
IT IS NEITHER CHASING NOR AVOIDING
BUT JUST BEING IN THE MIDDLE"

– Amit Ray (Indian author and spiritual master)

LESSON EIGHT: EQUINIMITY

People often describe me as calm and composed, which I am these days. If they'd have known me pre-2010, before I got sober and was introduced to The Twelve Step Program, calm is not an adjective they would have used to describe me. I was a whirlwind-chatterbox who turned into a Tasmanian Devil once I took an alcoholic drink. I was emotionally chaotic and mentally unmanageable, but I held it together well because I had my medicine (alcohol) to maintain the illusion of stability and control. The truth is, I'd not only lost control of my drinking, I'd lost myself, and those closest to me were starting to see through the cracks in my many masks. These days, however, I'm rarely obsessive-compulsive or unmanageable, rather, I am equanimous most of the time.

Maintaining equanimity (emotional balance, composure, calmness, self-control) under all conditions – despite difficulties – is one of the chief aims of leading a spiritual life, which essentially translates to being an honest, open, and loving person. An essential component of this maintenance is continuously observing your assets and liabilities with a real desire to learn about yourself and develop emotional intelligence by practicing unsparing self-survey. Wise people know that no one can make much of their life until self-searching becomes a regular habit; admitting and accepting what you find, building on the good, and patiently and persistently trying to correct what is hindering you.

'Emotional hangovers' are the direct result of yesterdays and sometimes today's excess of difficult emotions, especially shame. They can be avoided if we admit and correct our errors in the present, or soon after a mistake has been made. This is termed the 'spot-check inventory' in Twelve Step fellowships – where an error is recognized and amended on the spot. A spot-check inventory in the midst of emotional disturbances helps you overcome the daily 'ups and downs' of life, so you're not thrown too far off balance. Long-standing difficulties can be postponed for a time deliberately set aside to analyze them with a thorough 'moral inventory.' For the spot-check inventory to be effective you must have a willingness to admit your faults – in the moment – and forgive others when they are at fault. I've learned through this process of spot-check inventory that when I am disturbed by someone's behavior, there's actually something wrong with *me*. The other person may be 'in the wrong' but I can only deal with *my* feelings. When I'm hurt or upset, I have to continually look for the cause inside myself before I can admit then correct *my* mistakes. When I am free from internal disturbance, other people's behavior does not disturb me at all.

No matter how unreasonable others may seem, I am responsible for not reacting angrily. Regardless of what's happening around me, I'll always have the prerogative, and the responsibility, of choosing what happens within me. It's my responsibility to gain emotional balance and evolve my emotional intelligence. I must also stop judging others because none of us are perfect, and whoever is upsetting me is my best teacher. I've much to learn from him or her, as they hold up the mirror for me – so I can see what I need to change. Adele is my greatest teacher in this respect. She is what I call my 'Black Mirror,' as she reflects back to me all the things I need to change. I've had to learn to acknowledge her feelings and respond to her with empathy and compassion rather than react impulsively with condemnation or anger. Most importantly, when I feel I'm being criticized and my ego-alarm is activated, before my ego kicks-in to defend my position (with often critical or mean retorts), I've had to learn to pause and not 'get in the ring,' as my sponsor always advises me. Whenever I do get in the ring it never ends well; metaphorically

I get knocked-out every time!

Before sleep, draw up a balance sheet – ideally on paper, or a note on your SMART phone, tablet or computer. Close scrutiny will reveal your true motives in situations that happened throughout the day. This 'nightly inventory' will help balance you emotionally by crediting you with the things you've done well and acknowledging debts where due. Ask yourself these questions and answer honestly:

Was I resentful? Towards who and why?
Was I selfish? Why?
Was I self-seeking? Why?
Was I dishonest? Why?
Was I Afraid? Why?
Do I owe anyone an apology today?
Have I kept something to myself that should be discussed with another person at once?
Did I think today of what I could do for others?
Was I kind and loving towards all? Who especially?
What will I do differently tomorrow?
What am I grateful for today?

Rationalization and justification need to be put to one side when it comes to taking inventory; concentrate on the facts. Having honestly considered the events of the day, taking note of all the things you've done well, search your heart for any wish to hide bad motives underneath good ones. This subtle and elusive kind of self-righteousness can underlie the smallest act or thought and tends to permeate our relationships. Learning to spot, admit, and correct these flaws is the true essence of character-building and good living. An honest regret for harms done, a genuine gratitude for blessings received, and a willingness to try for better things tomorrow, are undoubtedly assets to develop that will evolve emotional intelligence and guarantee a happier existence.

Once this healthy practice has become part of your daily routine (much like brushing your teeth), you'll find self-examination so interesting and profitable that the time won't be missed. Nightly inventory will become a part of everyday living rather than something unusual and set-apart; most valuable because it helps you see that any time you're disturbed by a person, place, or thing, no matter what the cause, there's something wrong with *you*. If you are experiencing drama or stress, it's because you are creating drama and stress in your mind – due to not being emotionally balanced.

Anger, jealousy, envy, self-pity, and hurt pride, are emotional responses that can always be justified but ultimately, resentment and fear are the root of all these less-desirable reactions, and you are the person who hurts from carrying heavy emotions around. Getting it out of your psyche, by writing it all down, is the first step towards forgiveness of those people whom you have resentments toward, and seeing whom you might owe an apology and have to ask for forgiveness.

Through relationship counselling and reading a recommended book, *The Five Languages of Apology: How to Experience Healing in All Your Relationships* by Gary Chapman, I learned that making amends is not only saying sorry, it's admitting that you have done wrong and (in some cases) asking for forgiveness. A simple "sorry" will not suffice for most people when it comes to forgiving those who have wronged them because saying "sorry" is not actually admitting any wrong-doing. Admitting you are wrong does not mean you are bad or a failure, it is simply admitting that you made a mistake. Likewise, asking for forgiveness is not weakness, it is relinquishing control and putting the future of that relationship in the hands of the other person, which can be difficult. The mature and emotionally healthy individual is one who can recognize his/her wrongs, make amends, and ask for forgiveness (if necessary) despite the fear of rejection. We might feel we are at the mercy of the person we are asking forgiveness from (which is very common and makes us feel vulnerable). Historically, I found it almost impossible to admit my wrong-doing, especially to Adele, before I learned how to make amends through Twelve Step work and relationship counselling. I no longer associate being wrong with being a bad person, so I can admit when I am wrong and ask for forgiveness where necessary.

If the trust has been broken in a relationship, forgiveness is needed before the trust can be rebuilt. Forgiveness is a decision, whereas trust is an emotion. Trust is diminished if a person proves to be untrustworthy, therefore, a sincere apology and genuine forgiveness is needed to open up the possibility that trust can be rebuilt. Trust is the emotional sense that you can relax with a person and you don't have to be suspicious of them. You can let down your emotional guard because they will not knowingly hurt you, and this usually takes time (and returns in stages), especially if the trust has been broken. Trust is a normal emotional state in healthy individuals and healthy relationships.

The healthy individual will naturally trust until his/her trust has been broken, which is how Adele is programmed to operate. Those who have been deeply hurt in the past (especially in early childhood) tend not to trust until a person earns their trust, which makes inter-personal relationships more difficult to develop, as there is a lack of vulnerability. This is how I was programmed to operate, which makes life even more difficult as, "vulnerability is the underlying, ever present and abiding undercurrent of our natural state," according to English Poet David Whyte. Being vulnerable is being human.

Ultimately, it is a change in behavior over a period of time that enables a person to feel more comfortable and optimistic about the other person following an amend. If the new behavior continues, they will come to trust them fully again. This has been mine and Adele's experience since we rekindled our relationship in early 2018 after we split up in November 2017. Adele's trust in me took a long time to re-build, as I had left the relationship. There have been a series of arguments and amends that needed to be made before forgiveness could be granted and we had to learn a new language of apologies and forgiveness, so this has taken time and lots of effort.

Some relationships continue but they are not fully restored because there has been no forgiveness. The choice not to forgive usually pronounces the death penalty upon the relationship. Without forgiveness, relationships die. If forgiveness is not extended, then the apology hangs loose inside an already fractured system, and an apology alone cannot restore a relationship. An apology Is ultimately a request for forgiveness and forgiveness is the gift that repairs the relationship. However, forgiveness does not remove painful emotions or the memory of the event, as every event is recorded in the mind, so we never forget. Forgiveness, therefore, is a commitment to accept the person despite what he/she has done. It is ultimately a spiritual decision to show mercy.

Learning to practice self-restraint is a necessity, so you can develop patience and tolerance and not act rashly or hastily in any given situation. One unkind word or verbal tirade can ruin a relationship for a whole day, maybe even a whole year. Nothing pays off like restraint of tongue and pen (including SMS, emails, and social media messages). Avoid quick-tempered criticism and furious power-driven arguments, as they only cause more pain.

The same goes for sulking and silent scorn; these are emotional pitfalls baited with pride and vengefulness. When you're tempted by the bait, train yourself to pause, step back (don't get in the ring), and think, think, think, then the habit of self-restraint will become automatic, as you learn not to say the first thought that enters your mind. One should also be careful to practice self-control when achieving validation through some measure of importance or material success. Indulging in fantasies of greatness – especially victory over others – can lead to your friends turning away from you bored, or hurt, because you are blinded by prideful self-confidence and an out of control ego when you play the 'big-shot.' Remember that you're no better and no worse than anyone else. You are a unique human being but no more special than the next person, which is a humbling thought to continuously ponder and meditate on.

When you can see that all people, including yourself, are often to some degree emotionally unwell, and frequently wrong, you'll become more tolerant, patient, and truly loving of others. It's pointless to allow yourself to be hurt by people who, like you, are suffering from the pains of growing up. Most people would admit that it's very difficult to love everybody, but the idea of possessively loving a few and ignoring the many should be abandoned – if only a little at a time – as you grow toward altruism. Stop making unreasonable demands of those you love, and show kindness and compassion to those you don't know. With those you dislike, practice justice and courtesy, perhaps going out of your way to try to understand and help them where possible. Life will become so much easier. You can always ask yourself, "Am I doing for others what I would have them do for me?" And continuously affirm to your Higher Power in prayer, "Thy will be done, not mine."

"ALL OF HUMANITY'S PROBLEMS STEM FROM MAN'S INABILITY TO SIT QUIETLY IN A ROOM ALONE"

- Blaise Pascal (French mathematician, physicist and Catholic theologian)

LESSON NINE: CONSCIOUS CONTACT

Those who have come to make regular use of prayer, meditation, and mindfulness, would no more do without these practices than refuse air, food, or sunshine. If you deprive your body of such essentials, it will suffer. Likewise, if you turn away from prayer, meditation, and mindfulness, you are depriving your mind, emotions, and spirit of vitally needed nourishment. Nothing much can grow in the dark, so you'll need sunlight; meditation is your step out into the sun, which casts the light of awareness across the clouded thought-forms in the sky of Consciousness. Meditation is intensely practical, has no boundaries, can always be further developed, and one of its principle benefits is emotional balance. When self-examination, prayer, meditation, and mindfulness are practically interwoven, the result is an unshakable foundation for living life on life's terms. For this I can vouch.

Although there are many sceptics, there is also plenty of published scientific evidence to suggest that prayer changes neurotransmitters in the brain and can have a healing effect throughout the body. The positive results of prayer are beyond question. All those who persist find a strength not normally their own, wisdom beyond their usual capacity, and peace of mind that can stand firm in the face of difficult circumstances, which often take unexpected – even miraculous – turns for the better. Out of grief and suffering, new lessons are always learned, new resources of faith and courage are uncovered, and the conviction of the existence of a Higher Power is often cemented. "Faith is the surety of the omnipotence of God and man; the certainty that man will reach the deific life. Salvation is a ladder reaching from the heart of man to the heart of God. It has three steps; Belief is first, and this is what man thinks, perhaps, is truth. And faith is next, and this is what man believes is truth. Fruition is next, and this is what man knows is truth," according to Jesus Christ in Levi H. Dowling's *The Aquarian Gospel of Jesus the Christ*.

I would argue that conscious contact (deliberate connection) with a Higher Power is best achieved by praying and by learning a formal technique such as yoga, meditation/mindfulness, or mantras that induce the 'The Relaxation Effect.' I believe Consciousness is deep down within you in the blissful silence, therefore you need to be relaxed to commune with your inner-most self. The more regularly these techniques are practiced, the more deeply rooted the benefits will be, as you will come more in alignment with your Higher Power's will for you.

World-renowned medical practitioner, psychotherapist, and trainer of Acceptance & Commitment Therapy (ACT), Dr. Russ Harris, who is the author of the international best-selling book, *The Happiness Trap*, says, "Mindfulness can be defined in a variety of different ways, but they all basically come down to this: Mindfulness is a transformative mental state of awareness which involves focusing your attention with flexibility, openness, and curiosity. This simple definition tells us three important things. First, mindfulness is a process of awareness, not thinking. It involves paying attention to your experience in that moment as opposed to being caught up in thoughts. In a mindful state, you can let difficult thoughts and feelings freely flow through you, without getting caught up in them or pushed around by them, and without getting into a struggle with them. Second, mindfulness involves a particular attitude: one of openness and curiosity. Even if our experience in the moment is difficult, painful or unpleasant, we can be open to and curious about it instead of running from, fighting with or trying to avoid it. Third, mindfulness involves flexibility of attention: the ability to consciously direct, broaden or focus attention on different aspects of experience. We can use mindfulness to 'wake up,' connect with ourselves and appreciate the fullness of each moment of life. We can use it to improve our self-knowledge – to learn more about how we feel, think and react. We can use it to connect deeply and intimately with the people we care about, including ourselves. And we can use it to consciously influence our own behavior and increase our range of responses to the world we inhabit. It is the actions of living consciously – a profound way to enhance psychological resilience and increase life satisfaction."

A variety of meditation-based programs have been developed in recent years to reduce stress and medical symptoms, and to promote wellness. There are two widely used meditation-based stress reduction courses. One is based on the relaxation response first described by Herb Benson, MD, Director emeritus of the Benson-Henry Institute for Mind Body Medicine at Massachusetts General Hospital, which focuses on eliciting a physiologic state of deep rest – the opposite of the 'fight or flight' stress response. The other is Mindfulness-Based Stress Reduction, developed by Jon Kabat-Zinn, PhD, of the University of Massachusetts Medical School, which emphasizes a particular, non-judgmental attitude termed 'mindfulness' as being key to stress reduction.

The scientific philosophies and meditative traditions upon which each program was founded are different, and these differences are reflected in the instructions and exercises taught to patients. The programs' creators implied that each program promotes wellness through different mechanisms of action, which suggested the programs could potentially have different effects on mental and physical diseases. To investigate that possibility, healthy adults with high levels of stress were randomized to two eight-week programs; 18 completed the relaxation response program and 16 completed the mindfulness program. Both programs successfully decreased stress and increased mindfulness in participants, however, the mindfulness program resulted in further improvements in measures such as self-compassion and rumination – clearly indicating that the programs are not the same. To further understand the similarities and differences between the programs, the team measured brain activity during a meditation technique common to both programs – the body scan, in which attention is moved sequentially throughout the body to develop bodily awareness. While the relaxation response program instructs participants to deliberately relax each area of the body as they become aware of it, the mindfulness program (Vipassana) emphasizes mindful-awareness and acceptance *without any attempt to change anything;* accepting the body and mind *as it is.*

Brain imaging results of participants during the relaxation response and mindfulness programs showed that the strength of neural interaction between brain regions associated with present-moment awareness and bodily attention increased during both types of body-scan meditation, but each program also showed unique patterns of brain activity in line with the different theoretical orientation of each program. The relaxation response program works more through deliberate control mechanisms, while the mindfulness program works more through sensory awareness and perception mechanisms. It is analogous to weight training vs. aerobic exercise; both are beneficial but each has its unique mechanism and contribution. Further studies are being undertaken to determine whether these neural and psychological differences impact specific diseases in unique ways. I can attest that Vipassana has certainly helped me with the disease of addiction and my mental health issues in general. I am far less obsessive-compulsive and far less prone to substance and/or behavior binges since I began practicing meditation.

VIPASSANA

Vipassana is one of India's most ancient meditation techniques and a recognised science of the mind. Long lost to humanity, it was rediscovered by Gautama Buddha more than 2500 years ago. The word Vipassana means 'insight' (seeing things as they really are with one-pointed attention); a process of self-purification by self-observation. One begins by observing the natural breath to concentrate the mind then, with a sharpened awareness, one proceeds to observe the changing nature of body and ego-mind and experience the universal truths of impermanence, suffering, and egolessness. This truth-realisation – by direct experience – is the process of mental purification; eliminating 'sankhara's' (mental defilements) experienced in the body as physical discomforts and pains. The teaching of 'Dharma' (as it is known), is a universal remedy for universal problems and has nothing to do with any organised religion or sectarianism. For this reason, it can be freely practiced by anyone, at any time, in any place, without conflict due to race, community, or religion, and proves equally beneficial to everyone.

Although Vipassana was developed as a technique by the Buddha, its practice is not limited to Buddhists, and there is absolutely no question of conversion to Buddhism. The technique works on the simple basis that all human beings share the same problems and a technique which can eradicate these problems will have a universal application. This massively resonates with me because I have always claimed that humans universally experience the same emotional and mental health issues in varying degrees of severity; The Spiritual Malady. People from many religious denominations have experienced the benefits of Vipassana and have found no conflict whatsoever with their particular faith. Even though I was asked at the beginning of the retreat to put aside any rituals I might practice and any notion I might have of God, I felt even closer to my Higher Power than usual during the retreat, as I became more lovingly-aware of Consciousness.

Vipassana meditation aims at the highest spiritual goal of total liberation from suffering; Enlightenment. Its purpose is never simply to cure physical disease and mental illness, however, as a by-product of mental purification, many psychosomatic diseases are eradicated, which can result in seemingly miraculous cures of physical illnesses. Vipassana eliminates the three causes of unhappiness: craving, aversion, and ignorance. With continued practice, Vipassana can dissolve the stress and tensions developed in everyday life, untying the knots tied by the old habit of reacting in an unbalanced way to situations, which brings freedom, peace of mind, and contentment.

This process of self-purification by introspection is certainly not easy, and I feel that Vipassana will suit only those willing to work very seriously and observe the daily discipline. Continuity of practice in seclusion is the secret to the technique's success, which I find very difficult living in a house with Adele, three children, and my dog. Since returning from the Vipassana retreat, I've found that I simply don't have time to practice the recommended two hours per day. I usually manage 30-40 minutes (split into two sessions) and I have yet to go anywhere near as deep in meditation as I did on the retreat. However, I try to live my life mindfully and I still feel the benefits of the practice, as I am hardly ever unhappy despite often challenging circumstances in my life.

Thanks to Vipassana, I am certainly more equanimous and contented, and generally less fearful of responsibility, which has historically held me back from feeling fulfilled – and has prevented me from experiencing prolonged peace of mind. I even bought a puppy in February 2019, Teddy, who I love unconditionally with a love that deepens through my meditation practice. In fact, Teddy can often be found on my lap meditating (sleeping) with me in the morning, and I often experience moments of serenity when I'm out walking him mindfully in the open grasslands near my house.

My friend (and soul-sister) Kate has been on her spiritual journey since 2006. She experienced a Vipassana meditation retreat in 2014 and her first, life-changing ayahuasca ceremony in 2016. This is her story in relation to 'conscious contact'…

My boyfriend Luke met Ren at an ayahuasca retreat in Mallorca in 2017. I had previously been on the same retreat and following my experiences, Luke was prompted to follow. We have kept in touch with Ren and are delighted to call him our friend and brother since Luke experienced a beautiful bond with him whilst sharing a profound medicine journey together.

I recall a time when I first saw someone's ayahuasca experience on TV. It was English documentarian, indigenous rights advocate, author, explorer, trek leader and former Royal Marines commando officer, Bruce Parry. It shook me and made me feel scared and excited all at the same time; a feeling I remember vividly as being so strong… strong enough to know that someday, I too would be sitting with the medicine.

A friend of mine suggested that one is 'called' by the medicine and I believe this to be true. It is a feeling so strong and determined that you feel you have little choice but to step up and meet with Mother, Madre, or God (words used to describe the cosmic force that so many report meeting during their ayahuasca experiences).

I had butted off my own 'call' for as long as I could until the pull became too great. I booked to fly to Mallorca and experience two ayahuasca ceremonies on a two-night retreat. The night before my flight I couldn't sleep. I was so scared that I sat on the kitchen floor crying. Luke came in and said, "You don't have to go if you don't want to," but deep within me, I knew that there wasn't really a choice.

I set off armed with a question... a question that needed answering before I could continue my life with any sense of meaning. I had got to the point in my conscious awakening whereby I was irritable and frustrated. I had this deep inner knowing that I was here to do something, that this life couldn't just be this, that there was some kind of Higher Purpose; a mission that I had forgotten... I needed to know how I was here to serve.

During the weekend and under the influence of the medicine, I found myself in God, in the Mother. I also found her in me. I am not religious, I found something beyond that too. I found a purity of love so deep yet so simple. I understood such intelligence and divine orchestration and I knew that I belonged to it. I purged and stripped back plenty of rubble that was shielding me from seeing, knowing and feeling this pure love, this holding, this exquisite container.

I left feeling alive and aligned, with a feeling in my heart that I will never quite capture in words. Yet... I still didn't know why I was here and how I was to serve. My question hadn't been answered. Despite this, following the ceremonies, I had a feeling of wanting to do more, to share my learning and to serve in love and of connection with others. I knew I wanted to bring us back into harmony and alignment with our highest and greatest selves. I went home with a greater sense of love and patience with my question.

Three weeks later, it was my birthday. Luke handed me my very own drum. It became clear, not like lightening or some romantic version of the truth, but day by day an increasingly more vivid picture began forming in my head that I would drum in a circle of women along with other modalities to bring insights, connection and empowerment to women.

I seemed to just all of a sudden know that the rising of the feminine needed to come into balance on this planet in order for us to come back into alignment, and that my job was to do my part in enabling women to rise.

My project, 'Sister Circle,' was created on the summer solstice 2018 and has now grown to over 1000 women within my online community. I host circles, retreats and ceremonies for women. I had no idea this would be what I would be doing with me life, yet I already had all the skills which were needed. It turns out I had been training all my life. I am an eloquent speaker having taught as a drama teacher in my previous work-role. I trained in counselling and had been through many 'de-rubbling' processes myself. I taught challenging young people for ten years. I already knew how to offer information to others, how to inspire and guide a group. My experience was so easily transferred to planning and hosting the circles for women.

It's incredible to me that I had no idea my experience, that I like to call 'my training,' was exactly the skills and learning I needed in order to bring myself here, to Sister Circle to serve within this world. I will never again doubt the messy, winding, often incomprehensible path I might be on, and neither should you. Going with the flow is the biggest learning here; trusting in the Divine Flow and the Supreme Intelligence is the key to acceptance, inner peace and your closer connection to a Higher Power. There is a Taoist expression known as, 'Wu wei,' which refers to alignment with the natural flow of the universe. It is effortlessly softening to the way in which life wants you to go, trusting that every experience, every crisis, every grief, disappointment and closed door, every battle, victory and celebration is bringing you closer to the sacred, into meaning, into who exactly you are supposed to be and the story you will tell.

Often, my memory of my plant medicine experiences, the ayahuasca that lives in my veins and the heart-song I now know, fades. In order to retain my connection, I cultivated a regular practice of meditation and sacred ritual, so that I could always find myself close to the Great Mother. When I carve at these times during my day, light a candle, get out of my head and listen to her whispers within my heart, I cry with profound remembering. Yet when I am in my head, I can find myself in to-do lists, pushing forwards, doing, doing, doing, and in that doing I can easily forget my practice and the value to be found in that special half an hour. Yet It is the beautiful essence within my neglect and my mistakes that makes the remembering so beautifully profound.

I recall wanting a quick-fix from the many healing experiences I've had; demanding a revolutionary expansion or a radical removal of my layers of social and ancestral toxicity. I would arrive thinking 'just fix me' and then I can live happily ever after. From a Vipassana meditation retreat to extreme detoxes, from shamanic work to ancestral healing, from coaching to personal development practices and finally, after four ayahuasca ceremonies, now, I finally discovered – deep in my core – that ayahuasca and all other healing modalities, including groups and practices, are our guides, our container and our support system. Yet it's ourselves in our beautiful humanness with its spiritual epicenter that will move us, shake us and heal us. No one or anything external is going to truly fix us. They will be able to inspire, guide, coach and hold us whilst we release and rebuild but fix us, no.

To offer yourself to another to be 'fixed' is not empowerment of the self and these are not the rules of this delicious game of life. It is the searching and discovery of what we already have within us. It's our own power and the knowing that we will ultimately become our own saviour on our journey home; to ourselves and to our own hearts that will carry us along with grace.

Kate L

"WHEN BILL W. AND DR. BOB CONVENED THE FIRST A.A MEETING... IT WAS NOT ONLY THE BEGINNING OF THE SELF-HELP MOVEMENT AND THE BEGINNING OF THE INTEGRATION OF SCIENCE AND SPIRITUALITY AT A GRASS-ROOTS LEVEL, BUT ALSO THE BEGINNING OF THE COMMUNITY MOVEMENT... THIS MOVEMENT IS GOING TO BE THE SALVATION NOT ONLY OF ALCOHOLICS AND ADDICTS BUT OF US ALL"

– M. Scott Peck (American psychiatrist and best-selling author)

LESSON TEN: SERVICE

If you manage to put the previous nine lessons into practice, consistently, you'll be able to believe, feel, and do things that you were previously incapable of on willpower alone. You will truly move in a positive direction toward mastering your emotions rather than enduring them, and you will lay hold of a new Power that will transform you into a person with a greater degree of honesty, tolerance, and unselfishness; enjoying more contentment and peace of mind, exponentially. Not only that but you'll see people in a new light and develop the capacity to turn fear into love through compassion. Your mental horizon will broaden to include new narratives and you'll begin to notice things that you didn't previously notice, as every day will be offered to you in a new flavor – free from judgmentalism.

I believe spiritual awakening only comes to you if and when you are ready to become a different person. According to the late spiritual teacher and author Dr. Wayne Dyer, after the 'quantum shift' (spiritual awakening) happens, the top 5 moral ambitions for men change from material satisfactions to: spirituality, peace of mind, family, God's will, and honesty. And for women: personal growth, a sense of self-esteem, spirituality, happiness, and forgiveness. Friends and family of the spiritually awakened often find this change quite strange, as they don't understand why their friend or loved-one no longer conforms to the status quo, or why they question everything all the time, or why they want to be on their own in meditation. It can seem a bit odd, but introversion comes naturally to those who are 'awake,' as they tend to separate themselves from the crowd. It's mostly an unconscious choice; they don't deliberately ditch parties or gatherings, but their need to be alone transcends everything. While it may offend people who are close to them, it is necessary to maintain their equanimity and sanity.

I think my friends thought I was a bit odd in 2016 when I left the clubs in Ibiza in the early hours (after 'sober raving' all night) to go back to the hotel and meditate while they carried on partying. I needed my solitude away from the techno madness of DC-10, Ushuaia, and Space. When I'm alone in solitude with my Higher Power, I let my thoughts wonder into the shadowy crevices of my ego-mind where I come face to face with the truth. I learn much about my 'self' and the world that I did not know before. On the Vipassana retreat, for example, I learned that all fears stem from the ego-mind's fear of death, which is nothing more than an illusion because Consciousness, that gives rise to the ego-mind and the body, is eternal.

Once you are awake, you'll want to talk about more complex topics, as the universe begins to make more sense to you, but the majority of people won't understand. Some might even think you're a bit crazy but you'll learn not to care, as it's none of your business what others think about you. You'll also begin to trust your gut (intuition) more, as you know the universe has a plan – whether or not it may seem clear at the time. Not only this, but you will become conscious that you are trying to awaken other people too. This is about wanting to share great things, as you won't want to keep 'awakening experiences' to yourself – especially as you know they hold the power to heal humanity from The Spiritual Malady. As you become more in-tune with the universe, you'll notice signs everywhere, and all of life will become one great coincidence. Synchronicities will become more and more visible to you, which will help you continually evolve toward self-actualization/Enlightenment – whether you reach it or not.

Riding the train from Birmingham to London in August 2018, I had given Adele a box of 14 chocolates (7 each because 7 is my lucky number), which was the first of three gifts as part of my marriage proposal. My gaze was drawn to the digital clock on the ceiling of the carriage, it read 11:11. Many believers in 'New Age' philosophies have adopted the belief that the time 11:11 has mystical powers; 11:11 is supposedly a sign from the universe to give you evidence of your alignment. Some numerologists believe that events linked to the time 11:11 appear more often than can be explained by chance (or coincidence) and this belief is related to the concept of synchronicity. Some authors claim that seeing 11:11 on a clock is an auspicious sign, and others claim that 11:11 signals a spirit presence. In that moment, I certainly noted it as a potential sign of luck. 24 hours later the synchronicity was apparent when the favorable circumstances presented themselves.

The next day, Adele and I sat at a table in London's, The Savoy Hotel (Tea Room), having scoffed a platitude of finger sandwiches, awaiting our cakes and scones. Thirty minutes earlier, when we were seated by our maître d', I had handed Adele a present wrapped in Beauty and The Beast wrapping paper, as Beauty and The Beast is Adele's favorite Disney movie. Unbeknown to Adele, underneath the wrapping paper was a black box and inside the black box was a 'message in a bottle,' which read, "Dearest Adele, You deserve to be loved by a man who loves you before, during and after your morning tea – regardless of whether or not you've fussed over yourself in a mirror that day, a man who lovingly listens to how your day went and cracks a perfectly timed joke to get you out of your anxious head and back into your body, a man who understands that love is shown through the little things, a man who sees organizing your environment as an act of love in itself. I am this man and I love you. Marry me?"

Adele commented how nice it would be if the vacant ebony piano situated in front of us were to be played. Moments later a tall, slender, dark-haired woman dressed in black sat down at the piano and began to play. Adele immediately became emotional and exclaimed, "I don't believe it, this is my favorite song from Beauty and The Beast!" My head almost exploded at the synchronicity, or 'God-instance,' as I've come to understand it. My heart-rate increased rapidly. I uttered to Adele, "You can open your present now." As she read the message (with Beauty and The Beast's theme song playing in the background) I took the white box containing the platinum diamond engagement ring out of my pocket, got down on one knee, and asked Adele to marry me. By this point everyone in the room was observing the spectacle in silent anticipation, and when Adele said "Yes," we received rapturous applause from our audience, as we rose to our feet hugging and kissing.

That is just one example of my many amazing synchronicity stories that cannot be explained by reason, or as mere chance or coincidence. Once you have a spiritual awakening, you know intuitively that a Great Power – way beyond our current comprehension – is the basis of all our lives. Synchronicity seems to be one of its main modes of communication, especially in my life. Synchronicity might also be an indicator of predetermination, as everything in existence would be experienced as one continual event in motion from an omnipotent Higher Power's perspective. Christian theologian and Neoplatonic philosopher, Augustine of Hippo, wrote of this philosophy known as Eternalism, "God is outside of time." Catholic priest and philosopher, St. Thomas Aquinas, took the same view, suggesting that God would perceive something like a 'block universe,' with no objective flow of time, and time would appear differently to the finite beings contained within the universe. Time is merely a social construct, when in reality, *All is Now.*

On 'day 9' of the Vipassana retreat, after morning meditation, the talking sanction was lifted and we were allowed to communicate freely with one-another. The first person I spoke to came over to me and introduced himself as Alex. He was very forthright in telling me that the reason he'd come straight to me was because usually, in the outside world, he would never approach someone he considered an 'alpha-male' and rival to his ego, but because his ego had been deflated over the course of the retreat, he felt only love toward me and he wanted to connect, which is exactly how I felt about him. Synchronistically, it turned out we had lots in common. In fact, Alex reminded me of my younger self, as he was fifteen years younger and an aspiring DJ with relationship problems, which is exactly where I was aged 23. I gave him a lift home to Birmingham from Hereford, as he was about to start university in the city not far from where I live. On the drive home we connected on a soul level due to the depth of our empathy and compassion for each other following ten solid days of meditation.

The second person I spoke to, after the silence had been lifted, was a guy called Mark from London, who I also connected with on a soul level and, synchronistically, he was good friends with a guy I know from a Twelve Step fellowship in London. Mark and I are still in touch and I sometimes stay at his place when I visit London. Since the retreat, Mark has become a 'psychonaut,' who regularly 'trips' with 5-MeO-DMT from the venom of the Bufo alvarius toad, and he is training to become a kambo practitioner in order to help people overcome trauma in the same way he is doing for himself. Given my interest and experience with traditional medicines, it was no coincidence that we met.

One of the most significant people I spoke to was my room-mate Xavi, whom I had shared a room with for nine days in total silence. Our conversation started in the early evening and went on to the early hours of the morning, as we had so much in common. Specifically, our relationship issues, and that we had both had comparable spiritual experiences with the psychedelic plant medicine ayahuasca. Xavi was astonished that I made it through the retreat, as he had witnessed me suffering with a terrible head-cold and presumed I would have to quit. He recognized my stoicism and validated my achievement. The synchronicity of our situations reminded me of the interconnectedness of all people, as synchronicity essentially transcends reason and brings us directly onto the realm of Consciousness. I don't believe in coincidence because what seems to be coincidence is actually synchronicity, which, as Albert Einstein famously posited, is, "God's way of remaining anonymous."

Two months after the retreat, in November 2018, I was driving home from a Twelve Step meeting in the Midlands countryside and the thought came to me to check out the local Buddhist temple. I'd been meaning to do so for some time but this particular time felt paramount, as my intuition was so strong. I arrived and asked one of the monks if it was ok to have a look around. The monk introduced me to a young man called Ethan who showed me the meditation space and the Wat grounds. Synchronistically, Ethan was about to go on the same ten-day Vipassana silent meditation retreat in Hereford that I had been on only a few weeks prior to our meeting. This auspicious 'coincidicity' was not lost on either of us and I was able to answer his questions and put his fears to rest. I left the Wat, and as I admired the azure sky and startlingly beautiful white-gold sun hanging over the autumn-green fields on my drive home, I silently thanked my Higher Power for the experience.

Almost a year later, on the night of Adele's twenty-week scan, when we joyfully found out we were having a baby girl, I had another mystical and synchronistic experience when I was walking Teddy up a dimly lit path that transects the local common. To my surprise, two huge deer walked out from the dark forest to my right and crossed our path about twenty yards ahead. They stopped on the open grass to my left and surveyed us for about a minute before trotting into the trees. According to

Native American literature, "If a deer crosses your path, this only means that you are a gentle, compassionate, and loving person. When the deer totem enters your world, be prepared for new adventures and opportunities."

Once awakened, you'll begin to accept yourself as you are, and you'll accept others for who they are without judgement. Your awakening will propel you toward inner-peace and healing the world will become one of your long-term goals. Self-love will become more important to you, as you'll realize that you must make your mental, emotional, and physical health your No.1 priority. Materialistic things, validation, and success will interest you less and less. Trudging along in a job you have no passion for, earning as much money as possible and buying goods solely for the sake of it will not appeal to your soul. You'll gravitate toward your true calling – whatever that may be – and embrace it with open arms when the time comes. As you stand on the edge of new mysteries, joys, and experiences, no satisfaction is deeper, and no joy greater, than helping others – especially helping people to overcome their problems.

We all have problems and we can all find our way out of problems. It's only by accepting and solving your problems that you begin to get 'right' with yourself, and with the world around you. Furthermore, you now have the tools to deal with future failure, sickness, poverty, debt, bereavement, relationship issues, and loneliness, with faith and courage, as opposed to pride and despair. The humbler, more durable satisfactions in life will become more appealing, as peace of mind and contentment becomes your measuring stick for personal success. Monotony, pain, and misfortune can be turned to good use if you practice the spiritual principles discussed throughout this book.

Helping others will ensure an increasingly balanced emotional state and a more peaceful state of mind. Even though life might hand you problems when you least expect them, you'll have the resources to meet them without the need to escape or avoid them. With the help of your Higher Power you can take these problems in your stride, practice the principles of love and service in all your affairs, and use them as a source of growth and spiritual development, which will, in turn, inspire and afford comfort to those around you. When I was young, I was always told, "Life isn't fair," which I believe to be true, however, the spiritual life is the fairest life can be – simply because one learns to accept life *as it is*; totally indifferent to your desires, your aversions, and your ignorance.

As you grow spiritually, you'll learn that the satisfaction of your basic instincts and desires can't be the sole aim of your life. You'll therefore learn to temper and redirect your desires for emotional security and wealth, for personal prestige and power, and for sex. If you place selfish instincts first you will eventually be dragged back into disillusionment. Alternatively, if you're willing to place spiritual growth first, your attitude toward emotional security, and financial security, will commence to change profoundly, and you will develop stronger relationships with people because you won't try to dominate them, or be over-reliant upon them. Over-dependence upon people is unsuccessful because all people are fallible. Even the best of them will sometimes let you down, especially if your demands for their attention become unreasonable.

To feel emotionally secure, it's necessary that you learn to lead your life on a give-and-take basis, in partnership with all of those around you. Be willing to give your time to others – without demand for repayment. The more you do this, the more people will be attracted to you, and, as a result, the deeper and more vulnerable your interpersonal relationships will be. If you fail someone, they will understand, and if they fail you, you won't be seriously affected – and you can easily forgive them.

The best possible source of emotional stability is your Higher Power, which I hope by now you understand is *everything* including you. *You are God*. I don't mean this in a psycho-messianic kind of way, I mean *you are Consciousness* therefore you are God. As you develop more confidence and dependence on yourself, you'll safeguard an inner strength and peace that can't be easily shaken by the shortcomings of others, or any problem not of your own making. This positive mental attitude and optimistic outlook will teach you to have good relationships with others, and, as a result, you won't feel alone in the world. You can devote yourself to any number of ideas, enterprises, people, and constructive projects but money won't be a symbol of self-importance, as acquiring money will be an opportunity for service to those around you that makes for a serene and useful existence; performing humble labor without worrying about tomorrow. Money can simply be a means of pleasure by exchanging love and service with those around you – if you use it mindfully. Adele and I have been budgeting now for over two years. We've managed to pay for a wedding, honeymoon, family holidays, and save for our future, and the majority of money we spend is on our children rather than ourselves.

Contentment is not to be found in trying to be number one in terms of self-importance, wealth, or romance. Lasting happiness and joy come when you accept and play well with whatever cards you were dealt. What is material ambition really but the desire to be somebody, which is driven by the fear of being a 'nobody.' When you stay right-sized, you can still be ambitious but not absurdly so. Instead of material ambition, practice moral ambition. Reach beyond the desire for success and power towards the humble ambition to be of service to humanity. There is nothing wrong with ambition as a human quality providing the motive for success and validation is rooted in altruistic ventures that might benefit the many rather than the few.

All the great sages and mystics promise that once you learn how to master being peaceful, you'll be joyful and protected from everything that makes you feel anxious and depressed. In order to be at peace with the world, you must first be at peace with yourself. Through the natural maturing process of childhood and adulthood, most of the childish mentality is discarded and replaced by more appropriate coping skills. Some children, however, advance through the stages of physical growth without shedding many of their immature behaviors, especially those with adverse childhood experiences (ACE's). The 1998 ACE's study by Vince Felitti found that any child who experienced four or more of the recognized key areas of trauma (emotional abuse, sexual abuse, physical abuse, household substance misuse, living with a criminal member of the household, domestic abuse, divorce/separation, emotional neglect, physical neglect, or mental illness in the household) were four times more likely to be a high-risk drinker, six times more likely to have had or caused unintended teenage pregnancy, six times more likely to smoke e-cigarettes or tobacco, six times more likely to have had sex under the age of 16, eleven times more likely to have smoked cannabis, fourteen times more likely to have been a victim of violence, fifteen times more likely to have committed violence against another person, sixteen times more likely to have used crack-cocaine or heroin, and twenty times more likely to have been incarcerated at any point in their lifetime. ACE's, one might therefore argue, make it much more difficult for an adult-child to attain peace of mind and contentment.

When infantile traits continue into adulthood, the person is spoken of as 'immature,' and this immaturity is tied to feelings of omnipotence ('playing God' and needing to be in control), an inability to accept frustrations and personal criticism, having little or no patience, plus a range of characteristics, such as: fear of – and anger toward – authority figures; seeking approval that can lead to a loss of identity in the process; making good impressions but an inability to follow through; an addictive personality and often being driven to extremes; rarely satisfied and often immobilized by resentment; lonely even when surrounded by people; chronic complaining and blaming others for what's wrong in their lives; feeling like they don't fit in; perceiving the world as being filled with selfish people who aren't there for them; black and white thinking; living in the past while being fearful of the future; dependence and abandonment issues; fear of failure and rejection; an obsession with money and material satisfactions; an inability to tolerate illness in themselves or others; the belief that rules and laws are not for them; the holding-in of emotional pain and a loss of touch with their feelings. The Spiritual Malady on steroids no less! I think most people can relate to a few of these childish traits, in varying degrees, as most people have suffered some form of subjective trauma in their early childhood.

In a November 2016 interview with *The Sun* reporter Jeanne Supin, Psychiatrist and Senior Fellow of the Child Trauma Academy in Houston, Texas, Dr Bruce Perry stated, "Trauma is an experience, or pattern of experiences, that impairs the proper functioning of the person's stress-response system, making it more reactive or sensitive." According to somatic psychology, trauma symptoms are the effects of instability of the ANS (autonomic nervous system), as trauma disrupts the ANS. In recent years neuroscience has emerged with evidence that supports somatic psychology's opinion that the mind and body connection is deeply rooted, showing how the mind influences the body and the body influences the mind. Past traumas may manifest physical symptoms, such as pain, digestive issues, hormonal imbalances, sexual dysfunction, immune system dysfunction, depression, anxiety, and addictions, as our bodies hold on to the emotions of past trauma, which is reflected in our body language, posture, and expressions. Somatic psychotherapy can, therefore, return the ANS to homeostasis, and this therapy has been found to be one of the best ways to help patients suffering from psychological traumas to cope, recover, and live a normal life. This is where The Twelve Step Program has limitations in my opinion, and is the reason why I went for counselling and went through The Family of Origin program, and why I began experimenting with psychedelic medicines. Although the inventory process of Steps Four and Five is talking and feeling therapy combined, it did not go deep enough to remove all the stains of my trauma.

As we recover from trauma, emotional sensitivity, and immaturity, by walking a spiritual path, we become more aware of our limitations, our defects, our shortcomings, and our capabilities. I believe extreme childishness emerges as a reaction to feelings of shame and inadequacy, usually as a result of ACE's; most notably controlling, manipulative, and fearful behavior from parents, siblings, or friends, and a lack of unconditional love in those areas. Childish adults tend to be people-pleasers who strive for acceptance, meaning they seek things from outside of themselves to make them feel better, such as expensive clothes, fast cars, attractive partners, and adrenalin-rush excitement. Substances and behaviors are used as unwitting medications for their loneliness and emotional pain, as they attempt to fill the void with pleasure-seeking, power-seeking, and attention-seeking devices, but the void (The Spiritual Malady) always remains, and the cycle of 'fixing' continues, as I can attest. Even developing an attractive, charming, and magnetic personality to get their own way doesn't work, as no amount of status, money, fame, or love is enough for the scared little child inside to attain peace of mind or contentment. Driven by pleasure, attention, and power, the adult-child is over-friendly, charming, and manipulative – presenting a false impression to the world with many 'masks,' which protect them from being hurt. They most often control and dominate friends and partners, which is also a defense-mechanism to protect them from harm, as they don't want to experience similar emotional pain to that of their childhood.

As I've already mentioned, pain lives in – and travels through – families until someone is ready to accept it, feel it, and move past it. To overcome childishness, one must first recognize immaturity as the main problem to overcome. Immaturity is most often expressed as always being right and others always being wrong. The adult-child defends their 'rightness' at all costs, especially when they feel threatened, which continually reinforces the ego-mind's defenses and moves them further away from humility – giving rise to a feeling of omnipotence and being destined for greatness. Sadly, I have to admit that I relate to all of the above, as I am an adult-child of an alcoholic and my emotional growth was stunted when I started drinking alcohol aged 12. I only started to grow-up at the age of 28 when I stopped drinking, and this has been a slow and often painful process, as growing-up *is* painful. My life since 2009 has been a series of highs and lows with many new beginnings followed by many uncomfortable endings – on repeat – until I met Adele and finally 'settled down,' and started taking-on more responsibilities, as adults generally do.

Prior to recovery, I suppose I was always addicted to the thrill of success (in work) and the pain of failure (in relationships) in a masochistic kind of way; self-punishment and self-destruction always led to self-sabotage and never achieving my true potential. I was addicted to a life of ego-fueled excess and driven by feelings of low self-worth, which meant I was never satisfied with what I had, and I always felt frustrated or bored. This meant the euphoric and emotionally-suppressing effects of alcohol and drugs was exactly what my super-charged ego mind was always craving for. I had a tumultuous ten-year love-affair with 'chemicals.' Getting drunk and 'high' took over my life and became my main driver, as my excessive, aggressive, immature behavior increased progressively. My ego was like a raving maniac demanding to be fed, which is why I eventually became chemically dependent at 27 years of age.

Fortunately, I didn't join the infamous '27 Club' and a year later I was exhausted by my alcoholic lifestyle when I hit 'rock-bottom' the morning after my last alcoholic 'blackout' (when the brain's hippocampus switches off completely and stops recording memories due to a rapid increase in a person's blood-alcohol concentration). I woke up full of fear with no recollection of what happened the night before, or how I got to bed. The scared little child within me knew only one action to perform, and that was to get down on my knees and pray to a Father I didn't even believe existed. I surrendered. It was my first act of humility, and since that morning I've prayed every day and I have never taken another alcoholic drink. As a result, my life has progressively improved and I have steadily gained a deeper understanding of myself and my place in the universe.

I think those who seek a Higher Power are the ones who feel like something is missing. They have not had their emotional needs met in early life and, as a result, they seek something outside of themselves to make themselves feel better. This is where material pleasures and satisfactions often come in to play (until they stop working), then only a Higher Power will suffice. I suppose true wisdom is the realization that a Higher Power was inside them all along, deep down within. What I now know for certain is that the universe is alive and intelligent, and my purpose as a present, loving human being (continually being of service to my fellows) gives my life meaning, of which it was completely devoid prior to 'turning it all over' to my Higher Power. Everything I have in my life is a gift from The Organizing Principle. The only thing that is truly mine is 'my will,' which I gift back to my Higher Power every day. I turn my will and my life over to the care of my Higher Power and I ask instead for, "Thy will (to) be done."

No amount of egotism or material pleasures are substitutes for the happiness that is born out of my humble life. All I need are my Twelve Step community, my family, my friends, and my dog; everything else is a bonus, but I can take it or leave it, as more material satisfactions tend to bring more problems and they certainly don't bring lasting happiness. Love is the key ingredient. Without love for myself and others I couldn't be happy. However, love isn't something to simply profess, love is an action that must be demonstrated. With this in mind, I try to forget my selfish desires as often as I can, so I can spread love and share love with my family, friends, fellows, and colleagues. Love sets me free and it sets those I love free, as love is never possessive. If Adele wants to go out and do something without me, I encourage her to go and enjoy herself, and the same for the kids. All souls need to be free to live their own lives and find themselves. I believe we shouldn't impede a person's spiritual progress, we should only try to help them overcome their problems – if they ask for help.

Admittedly, it's not always easy to ask for help when we are going through tough times. I still go through periods when I get caught up in minor worries and stresses. It can feel like worrying and 'stressing-out' is the only available response to certain situations, but it definitely isn't. Serenity is not freedom from the storm, it is peace within the storm, and there are lots of proactive things we can do when the storm comes, such as: verbal connection (talking honestly with a fellow), prayer and meditation (time in solitude with your Higher Power), writing (taking inventory), creative expression (such as art or dance), physical exercise (if only a short walk), and most importantly being of service to others (maybe by volunteering).

Life will mean nothing if you keep pursuing meaningless things. The lasting happiness that is available for everyone is not a happiness of material satisfaction or pleasurable circumstances, rather, it is happiness through unbroken peace of mind regardless of circumstances. Peace of mind is always available in the present moment, but like any desirable state, it requires a bit of effort, even if that effort entails consciously choosing to do nothing and just be still for a while. There is no 'spiritual bypass' to peace of mind. If you haven't done the work on yourself you can't teach or help others to attain it. Awareness, therefore, is the key to accepting life's problems and attaining peace of mind and contentment, which is surely the purpose of living a human life? And if the purpose of a human life is to be contented by attaining peace of mind, I'd have to say the meaning of life must be to live a life full of meaning.

**"START WHERE YOU ARE.
USE WHAT YOU HAVE. DO WHAT YOU CAN"**

– Arthur Ashe (American professional tennis player)

LIFE IN RECOVERY

In 1993, American psychiatrist and best-selling author, M. Scott Peck wrote in *Further Along The Road Less Travelled*, "I've often thought that it would be saving if we could develop some program of mental health education in our public schools, but I know we wouldn't get away with it. People would object to it. There is an anti-mental health movement in this country (USA) consisting of people who are frightened by the influences of secular humanism and psychology movements in our lives... I hope someone will start instituting such a program. I also hope it will be done soon."

Generation after generation of altruistic individuals is surely a superior alternative to the continuation of selfish-self-seeking consumers perpetuating humanity's greed, jealousy, lust, anger, dishonesty, apathy, and fear? Many young people born in the 21st Century struggle to find aspirations other than being famous and making lots of money – usually both combined. Young people, like most adults, primarily wish to be happy but many don't know how to attain happiness because of fear, lack of clarity, lack of confidence, lack of self-esteem, and crucially, lack of knowledge. "It is no measure of health to be well adjusted to a profoundly sick society," according to Indian philosopher, Jiddu Krishnamurti. I would have to agree with him but I think it is possible to be a spiritual materialist; a person who appreciates material things but is not attached to them and their happiness does not depend on them.

As I have continually claimed throughout this book, there is no way you can fulfil yourself with material things because things are not capable of addressing your inner Spiritual Malady. I agree with Comedian and author Russel Brand's statement: "Addiction is rife because we are continually taught that we can fulfil ourselves, improve ourselves, advance ourselves with the acquisition of an external material object or through the validation or approval of other people. Wherever you are on the scale, if you're using an external object as a tool to ameliorate inner malady, you're engaged in addiction. Any behavior that you're engaged in that you want to change and when you try to change it or try to stop it, you can't, I think can rightly be referred to as an addiction." Addiction is the perfect metaphor for chronic material attachment, and materialism can never be a real measure of success because it does not bring lasting happiness. "To appreciate beauty and find the best in others, to leave the world a bit better, whether by a healthy child, a garden patch, a redeemed social condition, to know that someone has breathed life easier because you have lived, this is enough, this is to have succeeded," according to American philosopher Ralph Waldo Emerson, and I would have to agree.

While there is a great focus in our society on ambition, success, and academic achievement, there is a growing body of research demonstrating the positive impacts of social and emotional learning. The focus of most formal education systems is on teaching cognitive skills such as reading, writing, and arithmetic, but schools haven't changed much for hundreds of years – since they were designed to churn out factory workers. Teachers spend more time preparing young people for jobs that won't even exist in the future rather than investing more time in educating students on how to be holistically healthier, more helpful, and therefore happier human beings. The school set up is one of mass control and mass production, which, as far as I can tell, has at least five major problems:
1. Pupils have a lack of autonomy; every minute of the child's life is controlled by the education system. They are not in charge of their own lives, which means that many children get bored.
2. Memorisation and written learning is not authentic. Learning in schools is therefore inauthentic, and mostly useless

information is forgotten after exams. Schools only measure retention in a test culture.

3. Schools leave little room for passion yet pupils have unique interests and the key to fulfilment in life is finding our passions. There is no measure for how much potential is lost because schools are not designed to help children uncover what they are good at and what they want to do with their lives.

4. Schools punish slow learners yet pupils learn at different paces. If a child is a slow learner, they are often considered a failure.

5. Lecturing is the norm in schools but lecturing is a fundamentally dehumanising experience. Most classes hold around thirty children, who are forced to listen to one person and unable to interact with each other.

Thanks to the Internet, we now have access to all the information we will ever need. Technology has made it possible for anyone to learn anything. For fear of losing control, the education system is not leveraging this incredible resource anywhere near as well as it might. To prepare young people for the modern world, we need to fundamentally change the outdated education system, making it more engaging and more authentic. Life skills and character education should be paramount in my opinion, as scientific research shows that heart and mind learning are highly interconnected, and improving children's social and emotional skills directly benefits their ability to learn and apply cognitive skills.

According to the Dalai Lama Center for Ethics and Transformative Values at MIT in Massachusetts (USA), heart-mind wellbeing refers to creating a balance between educating the mind and educating the heart. We now know that for children to flourish socially and emotionally, we need to educate both their hearts and their minds. The significance of heart-mind wellbeing is:

- Children who develop social and emotional skills have better attitudes about themselves and others, and better social interactions.

- Children with strong social and emotional skills are less aggressive, can handle difficult emotions, and they have lower levels of emotional distress.
- Students who receive Social and Emotional Learning instruction improve an average 11 percentile points on standardized achievement tests compared to students who do not receive such instruction.
- We can successfully create conditions in schools, communities, and families that build the capacity of children to recognize their emotions, to understand and empathize with others, and to make constructive choices.
- We can foster positive human qualities such as compassion, empathy, and confidence, and we can help children manage difficult emotions such as fear, hatred, anger, and anxiety.

Research also reveals that the human heart is thousands of times more powerful and influential than the brain in sending signals and information to the rest of the body. The heart communicates with the brain and the body using hormones, the nervous system, and an electromagnetic field generated by the heart. The brain also generates an electromagnetic field, but it is much smaller and much less powerful than the heart field. The heart field envelopes the entire body and extends fifteen feet or more out into the surrounding environment. It has also been proven that our emotional state has a direct and powerful impact upon the heart, and this impact influences the quality of information sent by the heart to the brain. When our emotional state is one of inner peace, gratitude, contentment, and other positive feelings, the brain receives signals that promote the ability to focus, solve problems, perform physical and mental feats, and enhance creativity, intuition, and even spiritual awareness.

Heart-mind wellbeing consists of five positive human qualities, which are anchored in evidence-based research related to the social and emotional development of children:

1. Getting along with others; the ability to form positive and healthy relationships with peers and adults.
2. Compassionate and kind; the ability to be aware of other people's emotions and a desire to help when a person is in need.
3. Peaceful problem solving; the ability to behave in a peaceful and respectful way in a variety of situations and relationships.
4. Calm and secure; the ability to take part in daily activities and approach new situations without being overwhelmed with worries, sadness, or anxiety.
5. Alert and engaged; the ability to stay calm, focused and alert, and to demonstrate self-control by slowing down and thinking before acting.

Character education is an umbrella term loosely used to describe the teaching of young people in a manner that will help them develop as moral, well behaved, non-bullying, healthy, and socially acceptable human beings. Concepts that, now and in the past, have fallen under this term include: social and emotional learning, moral reasoning and cognitive development, life skills education, health education, violence prevention, critical thinking, ethical reasoning, and conflict resolution and mediation. Many of these, such as religious education, moral education, and values clarification are now considered failed programs. Today, there are dozens of character education programs in, and vying for, adoption by schools and businesses. Some are commercial, some non-profit, and many are uniquely devised by states, districts, and schools. A common approach of these programs is to provide a list of principles, pillars, values, or virtues, which are memorised – or around which themed activities are planned. It's commonly claimed that the values included in any particular list are universally recognized, however, there is no agreement among the competing programs on core values (e.g. honesty, stewardship, kindness, generosity, courage, freedom, justice, equality, and respect) or even how many to list. There is also no common or standard means for assessing, implementing, or evaluating programs.

I believe that Health Education (and Sex Education) in the USA and Personal, Social, and Health Education (PSHE) in the UK are programs that afford the perfect opportunity to instil new measures to treat emotional disorder, evolve emotional intelligence with heart-mind learning, and prevent the onset of mental illnesses that can lead to substance and behavioral addictions. It was written in A.A's *Grapevine Magazine* in March 1958, "The answer to the problem of alcoholism seems to be in education – education in school rooms, in medical colleges, among clergymen and employers, in families, and in the public at large... This means factual education, properly presented. Heretofore, much of this education has attacked the immorality of drinking rather than the illness of alcoholism... Now who is going to do all this education? Obviously, it is both a community job and a job for specialists. Individually, we A.A's can help, but A.A as such cannot, and should not, get directly into this field. Therefore, we must rely on other agencies, on outside friends and their willingness to supply great amounts of money and effort."

Working closely with members of local government in my role as a Team Leader for the Homeless Team of the UK's leading substance misuse service in one of the UK's largest cities, I have my finger close enough to the cultural pulse to measure why society is becoming increasingly sicker. It is very clear to me that the sickest members of our society are those people who have been the most traumatised. "Not everyone who is traumatised becomes an addict but every addict has been traumatised," according to Dr. Gabor Maté; a statement with which I wholeheartedly concur.

I proposed in my first book, *Addiction Prevention: Twelve Steps To Spiritual Awakening*, that substance and behavioral addictions are a symptom of emotional disorder (The Spiritual Malady) that develops into mental illnesses, which people attempt to medicate. Inadvertently, however, substance abusers often poison their brains and warp their minds further into profound mental illness due to prolonged substance misuse. Also, engaging in addictive behaviors, such as gambling, sex, exercise, shopping, and over-eating is mentally and emotionally damaging and detrimental to inter-personal relationships. Poor emotion management abilities and a lack of emotional intelligence can also lead to unwholesome (often destructive) relationships and progressively diminishing self-care.

I also suggested in the book that a growing number of children are presenting with symptoms of The Spiritual Malady long before they reach teenage years; symptoms that are often diagnosed as conditions such as: Conduct Disorder (CD), Attention Deficit Hyperactivity Disorder (ADHD), and Oppositional Defiant Disorder (ODD). More often than not they are often pharmaceutically medicated by GP's, which I feel is analogous to placing a small Band-Aid over a gaping wound.

As a member of Twelve Step fellowships, I am unable to further the ideas outlined in my aforementioned book to make them become a reality. I hope one day someone will use my blueprint and establish Twelve Step classes combined with heart-mind education in schools, as I have no doubt this would help bring about positive change in the lives of many young people. I believe The Program is comprehensive and unrivalled in terms of teaching a simple set of moral principles to live one's life by.

The Twelve Step Program is widely accepted as an effective treatment for emotional and mental illnesses. Over 200 self-help organisations – known as Fellowships – with a worldwide membership of millions, now employ The Program. About twenty percent of Twelve Step fellowships are for recovery from substance addictions, the other eighty percent address a variety of behavioral problems from debt to depression. For groups not related to substance abuse, the physical manifestation includes – but is not limited to – emotional and psychological issues such as: compulsive hoarding, distractibility, eating disorders, dysfunctional enabling, hyperactivity, hypomania, irritability, lack of motivation, laziness, mania, panic attacks, psychosomatic illnesses, poor impulse control, procrastination, self-injury, and suicide attempts.

Having been sponsored through The Twelve Step Program in 2010, I turned my life around and have since continued to practice The Steps in my daily life. I am, as a result, convinced The Program can be used to treat The Spiritual Malady in young people and possibly prevent future substance and/or behavioral addictions. I would also argue that practicing The Steps would be beneficial for all people – in terms of improving their mental health and general wellbeing. I couldn't agree more with Russell Brand, who wrote in his book *Recovery: Freedom From Our Addictions*, "The 12 Step program, which has saved my life, will change the life of anyone who embraces it. I have seen it work many times with people with addiction issues of every hue: drugs, sex, relationships, food, work, smoking, alcohol, technology, pornography, hoarding, gambling, everything. Because the instinct that drives the compulsion is universal. It is an attempt to solve the problem of disconnection, alienation and tepid despair, because the problem is ultimately 'being human' in an environment that is curiously ill equipped to deal with the challenges that entails. We are all on the addiction scale."

The Steps are not designed to be intellectualized. They are a simple program for complicated people, designed to be taken as a treatment for emotional disorder and the prevention of mental health issues that people attempt to medicate with substances and/or behaviors. The following is my proposed Twelve Step Program for Young People:

1. We admitted we were powerless over people, places and things – that our lives can be unmanageable.
2. Came to believe in a Power greater than ourselves.
3. Made a decision to turn our will and our lives over to the care of our Higher Power.
4. Made a searching and fearless moral inventory of ourselves.
5. Admitted to our Higher Power, to ourselves, and to another human being the exact nature of our wrongs.
6. Were entirely ready to have our Higher Power remove all these defects of character.
7. Humbly asked our Higher Power to remove our shortcomings.
8. Made a list of all persons we had harmed, and became willing to make amends to them all.
9. Made direct amends to such people wherever possible, except when to do so would injure them or others.
10. Continued to take personal inventory, and when we were wrong, promptly admitted it.
11. Sought through prayer and meditation to improve our conscious contact with our Higher Power, praying only for knowledge of His/Her/Its will for us and the power to carry that out.
12. Having had a spiritual awakening as the result of these steps, we tried to help others, and to practice these principles in all our affairs.

The evidence from a 2018 study by Public Health England (PHE) on 'Improving mutual aid engagement' shows that clients, who actively participate in mutual aid (community groups, such as Twelve Step fellowships), are more likely to sustain their recovery. Key evidence includes: "mutual aid has an extra effect when combined with structured treatment, it can reduce rates of post-treatment relapse and representation by providing a continuing support structure," and, "the addition of just one abstinent person to a drinker's social network increases the probability of abstinence in the next year by 27 percent." I have no doubt, therefore, had I been through The Twelve Step Program in my youth, I would have been more emotionally equipped with the knowledge and tools that are essential to avoiding the pitfalls of mental health issues and addiction, and discovering one's life purpose.

My vision is: The Twelve Step Program for Young People would consist of twelve weekly groups/classes; one Step completed per week. Participants would have a homework assignment related to each step, which they would hand-in the following week to be marked by the facilitator/teacher. For instance, for Step One, following a detailed presentation of powerlessness and unmanageability and a group discussion, participants would then be required to write down ten examples of powerlessness and ten examples of unmanageability in their lives as a homework assignment.

For Step Two, participants would be asked to write down ten reasons why they are not God, and for Step Three, write down as many ideas that come to mind about what a Higher Power might be for them. A Power they would be comfortable turning to, especially in times of need. Step Four would be the 'moral inventory,' the 'fear inventory,' and the 'sex inventory,' as outlined in the book *Alcoholics Anonymous*, and Step Five would be sharing this inventory with a trusted friend, teacher, mentor, or sponsor. Step Six would look at defects of character and Step Seven how to 'turn them over' to a Higher Power. Step Eight would look at making amends and Step Nine would be the making of those amends. Step Ten would look at taking daily inventory. Step Eleven would look at prayer, meditation and mindfulness. Step Twelve would look at altruism and being of service to humanity.

Unlike alcoholics, young people would neither be recovering from a seemingly hopeless state of mind and body, nor would they be sharing 'war stories' of substance misuse, but regular groups (or meetings) would help young people to gain a better sense of morality and share their worries and problems. Participants would most likely be sharing about affirmative action and how practicing the principles of love and service in their daily lives helps them overcome anxiety, pain, and adversity. They might also share about how they are being taught to manage negative feelings with healthy actions – instead of using substances and/or behaviors to change the way they feel or avoid feelings altogether. Meetings, therefore, might grant participants the liberty they so often desire but feel they are not permitted at school or in their home environment. Meetings would be essential to remind young people why they are continuing to work The Steps and prevent them from deviating from the spiritual path. They would also be a place to connect with fellows, share problems, be of service, and hear messages of hope. The Twelve Step way of life would cement young people with a healthy and unshakable foundation of faith, values, morals, and decency, upon which to build purposeful, prosperous, and productive lives.

If you feel my vision is too utopian, please bear in mind that I have witnessed young offenders go through a similar process when I worked in UK prisons, which helped many of them to change and begin to overcome past trauma.

For many young people today, their experience of life is something approaching a 'dystopia'; a deeply flawed, unequal society in which power, wealth, fame, and popularity are the measures of a worthwhile existence. It could be argued that this downward spiral can be blamed on political agendas but what I can say for sure is that for those young people whose life chances were slimmer straight from birth, their daily experience is often the misery brought about by poverty, lack of opportunity, childhood trauma, addiction, and the problems of the adults around them.

The challenges are getting greater in a society where the gap between rich and poor is ever-widening, where budgets for mental health and substance misuse services are continually being cut due to austerity, where housing is a lottery, where hate and crime is on the rise, where obesity is at a critical level, where young people are groomed by drugs gangs, where new psychoactive substances continually emerge onto a thriving market, and where young people can now buy drugs on the internet and have them home-delivered. For young people to learn to cope with a complex society that is clearly in trouble, it is vitally important that we teach them resilience from an early age and emotional coping skills that will equip them to meet future challenges. We must also teach them to recognise the difference between good and bad relationships, teach them why it is a good idea to look after themselves (and each other), and teach them to nurture themselves, their communities, and the environment, so they might grow into holistically healthy adults. There is not, and never will be, a technological solution to all these problems. The answer therefore lies in moving away from nihilism toward faith, and finding meaning and purpose in life through communication, prayer meditation, and mindfulness – under the umbrella of connection.

According to Austrian neurologist, psychiatrist, Holocaust survivor, and founder of Logotherapy, Victor Frankl, existential crisis is typical of modern societies in which people do what they are told to do, or what others do, rather than what they want to do. They often try to fill the gap between what is expected of them and what they want for themselves with economic power or physical pleasure, or by numbing their senses (with substances and/or behaviors). It can even lead to suicide. Discovering one's purpose in life helps an individual fill the existential void according to Frankl. We don't create the meaning of our life, as French philosopher Jean-Paul Sartre claimed, we discover it. Existential frustration arises when our life is without purpose, or when that purpose is skewed. However, rather than be seen as a negative, this frustration can be viewed as the catalyst for change.

All therapies are designed to facilitate change, but for me, CBT (Cognitive Behavioral Therapy) should stand for 'Coping Behavior Therapy' because it teaches you to cope with mental illness rather than overcome it. Logotherapy, on the other hand, offers a solution to our dis-ease because it does not see existential frustration as mental illness – the way other forms of therapy do. Rather, existential frustration is considered 'spiritual anguish' (The Spiritual Malady) in Logotherapy – the same as in Twelve Step fellowships. It is a natural and beneficial phenomenon that drives those who suffer from it to seek a cure, and in so doing to find greater satisfaction in life and change their destiny.

Having lived through this 'spiritual anguish,' and found a solution in a Higher Power (of my own understanding) thanks to Twelve Step fellowships, I changed my own destiny – from a possible future of jails, mental institutions, or death – to becoming a father, sponsor/mentor, philosopher, author, Team Leader, and podcaster. By learning to follow my intuition (my Higher Power's will), I discovered my life purpose and I now live a life beyond my wildest dreams, which has led me to attaining peace of mind and contentment, and enjoying a happy and joyful life in recovery.

RESOURCES

1. Alcoholics Anonymous
Author: Bill W and friends
Publisher: Ixia Press

2. Chasing The Scream: The First and Last Days of the War on Drugs
Author: Johann Hari
Publisher: Bloomsbury Publishing

3. Further Along The Road Less Travelled
Author: M. Scott Peck
Publisher: ocket Books

4.https://twitter.com/ssparklesdaily/status/4392419676589916
16?lang=en
Author: Stephanie Sparkles
Publisher: Twitter

5. Aghora: At the Left Hand of God
Author: Robert E. Svoboda
Publisher: Rupa Publications India

6. Pointers From Ramesh Balsekar
Author: Gautam Sachdeva
Publisher: Yogi Impressions Books Pvt. Ltd

7. HOLY BIBLE: King James Version (KJV)
Author: Tbd
Publisher: Collins

8. https://www.youtube.com/watch?v=b2emgrRoT2c
Author: Dr. Ken McCauley
Publsiher: Youtube

9. The Case Against Reality: How Evolution Hid the Truth from
Our Eyes
Author: Donald. D Hoffman
Publisher: Allen Lane

10. https://quantumenigma.com/nutshell/notable-quotes-on-
quantum-physics/
Author: Eugene Wigner
Publisher: quantumenigma.com

11. https://en.wikiquote.org/wiki/MaxPlanck
Author: Max Plank
Publisher: Wikipidea

12. Conscious: A Brief Guide to the Fundamental Mystery of the
Mind
Author: Annaka Harris
Publisher: Harper

13. Title:https://www.robertlanza.com/biocentrism-how-life-
and-consciousness-are-the-keys-to-understanding-the-true-
nature-of-the-universe/
Author: Dr. Robert Lanza
Publisher: robertlanza.com

14. https://en.wikipedia.org/wiki/Akashic_records
Author: Wikipedia
Publisher: Wikipedia

15. https://medium.com/@dilanka/psychedelic-experience-is-only-a-glimpse-of-genuine-mystical-insight-but-a-glimpse-which-can-be-e329f8df8bd6
Author: Alan Watts
Publisher: medium.com

16.http://www.adishakti.org/_/shakti_realm_of_the_divine_mother.htm
Author: adishakti.org
Publisher: adishakti.org

17. https://yogafreedom.org/2014/08/03/how-to-stop-judging-ourselves-others/
Author: Dilgo Khyentse Rinpoche
Publisher: yogafreedom.org

18. https://www.samaritans.org/about-samaritans/research-policy/suicide-facts-and-figures/
Author: Samaritans
Publisher: samirtans.org

19. https://www.biu.ac.il/HU/$source-next/hu/pele/man-condition/kant/en-enlight.htm
Author: Immanuel Kant
Publisher: www.biu.ac.il

20. The Aquarian Gospel of Jesus the Christ
Author: Levi H. Dowling
Publisher: Digireads.com

21. The Five Languages of Apology: How to Experience Healing in All Your Relationships
Author: Gary Chapman
Publisher: Northfield Publishing

22. Vulnerability
Author: David Whyte
Publisher: Onbeing.org

23. Mindfulness-Based Stress Reduction
Author: Jon Kabat-Zinn, PhD,
Publisher: New World Library

24.https://www.treatment4addiction.com/rehab/therapy/somatictherapy/
Author: Treatment 4 Addiction
Publisher: American Addiction Centers, Inc

25. https://childtrauma.org/wp-content/uploads/2016/12/Sun-Interview-Bruce-Perry-Nov-2016.pdf
Author: Jeanne Supin
Publisher: The Sun

26. https://www.psychologytoday.com/gb/blog/resolution-not-conflict/201603/can-you-spot-10-signs-childish-adult
Author: Susan Heitler Ph.D.
Publisher: www.psychologytoday.com

27. https://www.wildmind.org/blogs/quote-of-the-month/krishnamurti-measure-of-health
Author: Jiddu Krishnamurti
Publisher: www.wildmind.org

28. Heart Wisdom Podcast Ep 100 Love & Impermanence
Author: Jack Kornfield.
Publisher: Heart Wisdom Podcast

29. https://www.nbcnews.com/news/us-news/students-are-being-prepared-jobs-no-longer-exist-here-s-n865096
Author: NBC News
Publisher: www.nbcnews.com

30. https://www.ncfe.org.uk/blog/five-foundations-of-character-education
Author: ncfe.org.uk
Publisher: www.ncfe.org.uk

31. The Joe Rogan Experience Episode 1379
Author: Ben Westhoff
Publisher: The Joe Rogan Experience

32. The Mindful Way
Author: John Shearer
Publisher: Self-published

33. Ikigai: The Japanese secret to a long and happy life
Author: Héctor García
Publisher: Hutchinson

34. https://www.metaphysics-for-life.com/heart-mind.html
Author: metaphysics-for-life
Publisher: metaphysics-for-life.com

35. https://dalailamacenter.org/about/heart-mind
Author: dalailamacenter.org
Publisher: dalailamacenter.org

36.https://assets.publishing.service.gov.uk/government/uploads/system/uploads/attachment_data/file/769246/Improving-mutual-aid-engagement.pdf
Author: Public Health England
Publisher: service.gov.uk

Visit **www.lifeinrecovery.co.uk** for more book titles by
Ren Koi and his Life in Recovery Podcast

facebook.com/RenKoiLiRP

twitter.com/RenKoiLiR

instagram.com/renkoi_lifeinrecovery

DWYCtoday Publishing, Birmingham, United Kingdom. 2020

www.ingramcontent.com/pod-product-compliance
Ingram Content Group UK Ltd.
Pitfield, Milton Keynes, MK11 3LW, UK
UKHW021650190726
13853UKWH00001B/163